Gerald
Oct.
Columbia Univ.

POEMS BY EMILY DICKINSON

E. Dickinson.

Poems by
EMILY DICKINSON

EDITED BY
MARTHA DICKINSON BIANCHI
AND
ALFRED LEETE HAMPSON

Introduction by
ALFRED LEETE HAMPSON

BOSTON
LITTLE, BROWN AND COMPANY
1948

Published February, 1937
Reprinted December, 1938
Reprinted November, 1939
Reprinted April, 1941
Reprinted September, 1942
Reprinted August, 1943
Reprinted February, 1944
Reprinted August, 1944
Reprinted December, 1945
Reprinted October, 1946
Reprinted April, 1947
Reprinted April, 1948

PRINTED IN THE UNITED STATES OF AMERICA

INTRODUCTION

EMILY DICKINSON was born December 10th, 1830, lived her life apart, and died May 15th, 1886, in the same little college town of Amherst, among the Massachusetts hills, where her grandfather, Samuel Fowler Dickinson — a "poet" and mystic of another sort — had ruined himself for the materializing of his apocalyptic vision: the founding of Amherst College, which he foresaw as "an agency to hasten the conversion of the whole world."

Unknown during her lifetime, held by an intimate public in peculiar affection after her death as her first posthumous publications reached an outside world, later neglected for many years by public and critics alike and classified in 1912 as "a forgotten poetess", her present eminence is a special triumph, unique in the annals of American letters. Though her period coincided with the Golden Era of New England literature, "her fame, as pure poet, has outgrown that of every contemporary."[1] "She seems to many of us the greatest American poet of the Nineteenth Century."[2] "A modern of moderns" in 1936, critics on both sides of the Atlantic do not hesitate now to call her poetry, wholly underivative, "the finest by a woman in the English language." "Her influence, negligible at first, is now incalculable."[3]

By inheritance Emily Dickinson was the quintessence of New England. Of Norman origin, the name de-

[1] *American Literature, An Introduction;* p. 68. Carl Van Doren.

[2] *New York Herald Tribune,* September 27, 1936. (XIII–p. 6.) Lewis Gannett.

[3] *Modern American Poetry* (fifth revised edition). Louis Untermeyer.

riving from Gautier of Caen (anglicized as Walter de Kenson) who accompanied William the Conqueror in the invasion of England, her first Colonial ancestor was the picturesque and indomitable Nathaniel, whose spirit of adventure — as well as his Puritan political convictions — led him to set sail in 1630, with his wife Anna, "the widow Gull", for the wilds of America, seeking "not conquest or dominion, but freedom and the right to serve, at the dictation of his own conscience, his God before his King."

With a few others, they soon struck out for the hinterland, leaving the comparative security and companionship of the coast settlements which retained, bleak outposts though they were, a tenuous connection with their old world, and eventually established the town of old Hadley, Massachusetts, some of their descendants crossing the Connecticut river to occupy the district later called Amherst. Faced by primeval conditions of incredible hardship, surrounded by wild beasts and Indians, these uncompromising idealists wrought out their own Colonial history in blood and shining courage.

Just two hundred years lay between the birth of Emily Dickinson and the coming of her first ancestor from England. She shared with the other children of her village the prevailing traditions and standards of her time. Her father, educated at Yale, followed the family profession of law, served in the State Legislature and also in Congress, and was Treasurer of Amherst College for nearly forty years. Although habitually reserved in manner, he evidenced the marked individuality and love of independence characteristic of the Dickinsons from the beginning, as well as — under provocation — their proclivity for vivid and original expression. "If Father is asleep on the lounge the house is full", Emily exclaimed. It revealed their fundamental understanding.

The general rise of affluence felt throughout New England in the 1830's was enjoyed by the Dickinsons, and Edward Dickinson was never happier than when dispensing the somewhat stately hospitality of his home, beaming welcome upon his guests and pride in the dainty wife beside him — a lady of the old school long passed into mythology — whose dower of claw-footed and pine-apple-cut mahogany and flower-basket silver had been brought by yokes of oxen over the hills upon their marriage in 1828. The reverses that bore down upon him all too soon were the result of his generosity and taking upon himself the obligations of others, only to be surmounted by years of self-denial and painstaking effort.

There was no exception to what was expected of any one of the three children — Emily, or her brother Austin and sister Lavinia — all of them possessed of marked ability and varied temperament. Helen Fiske, the daughter of Professor Fiske, and later to be famous as "H. H." (Helen Hunt), the author of *Ramona,* was their favorite playmate. When Emily was sixteen she met Susan Gilbert, just nine days younger than herself, who was to be her brother's wife — and to become the most comprehending and mentally stimulating influence in her own life.

Emily attended Amherst Academy, and was for a year a student at Mary Lyon's Female Seminary at South Hadley. As shown in the family letters and diaries of that period, the Dickinson house overflowed with young life, Emily playing a vivid part in it all, giving no hint of her later seclusion. She made visits in Worcester and Boston, and in 1854 when her father was a member of Congress went to Washington, where her wit and intelligence were quickly remarked.

It was during the visit in Philadelphia on her way home, that, in the words of her closest contemporaries,

"Emily met her fate."[1] According to them, two predestined souls recognized each other, — the man a powerful preacher, a scholar, a poet, already married. The inevitable renunciation followed. Its effect, however, was to be enduring. For Emily, all had no codicil. In the old familiar places and ways she took up her life again, not choosing to withdraw from the world — at least not all at once nor definitely at first — but gradually, irresistibly, as her own work and premonition drew her. Her poems became her absorbing passion, those poems from whose publication she recoiled, and which were only made known to the world after her death.

Not until 1890 did a selection of these poems appear, made available by her sister Lavinia, to be followed shortly by two additional selections. Many years later, in 1914, her niece, Martha Dickinson Bianchi, presented another volume entitled *The Single Hound,* composed of poems written by Emily Dickinson to "Sister Sue", her brother's wife. The war intervened, and in the deluge of free verse which followed, Emily Dickinson was submerged. For a decade nothing more was published. The critics, and the general public as well, left her to the devotion of her self-styled initiates.[2]

Undeterred by the apathy of public and publishers, however, these enthusiasts imposed it as a duty upon her niece — as the only surviving member of the family, who had lived beside her day by day — to give them some actual re-creation of the poet as a woman, and of her unique background. The *Life and Letters*[3] was, therefore, presented in 1924. Its reception was an overwhelming surprise. Written at the instigation of and for a limited special public already steeped in her po-

[1] See *Emily Dickinson Face to Face,* Martha Dickinson Bianchi, Houghton Mifflin Company; pp. 48–53.

[2] See *Foreword* to *Emily Dickinson Face to Face;* pp. ix–xiii.

[3] *The Life and Letters of Emily Dickinson,* Martha Dickinson Bianchi, Houghton Mifflin Company.

etry — to help them see the flesh-and-blood Emily as she moved about in her own setting, it interested as well an entirely new public that had never known her work. There was an immediate demand for a collected edition of her poems, thought then to be the *Complete Poems,*[1] which was supplied as rapidly as possible to companion the *Life and Letters,* being published four months later. Suddenly Emily Dickinson became a figure of international importance.

The thorough overhauling and minute examination of the papers and letters of three generations of Dickinsons which inevitably followed, resulted in the discovery and the publication in 1929 of the *Further Poems*[2] (which in 1930 were included in the *Centenary Edition*[3]), and of the *Unpublished Poems*[4] in 1935. The former caused a literary sensation. "No other recent book can be so important to American Literature", in the *Atlantic Monthly;* "Places Emily Dickinson indubitably and permanently among the enduring poets of the English speaking race", in the *New York Times;* and "Colossal Substance" in the *Saturday Review of Literature,* typify the critical consensus at this time. The "forgotten poetess" of 1912 was now acclaimed thus by Mark Van Doren in the *Nation:* "Emily Dickinson is much the best of women poets and comes near the crown of all poetry."

The *Unpublished Poems,* appearing fifty years after Emily Dickinson's death, were "but further proof that she is of the immortals", according to Percy Hutchison in the *New York Times Book Review.* "In this libation there are no dregs, no single drop can be spared", is the conclusion of William H. McCarthy in the *Yale Review;* while in the *American Mercury* Louis Unter-

1, 2, 3, 4 Little, Brown and Company. A limited edition of the *Unpublished Poems* appeared in November, 1935, the trade edition in February, 1936. These poems are reprinted at the end of this book under "Additional Poems."

meyer asserts that the reader can only be grateful for more of the audacious images and dazzling communications "which make Emily Dickinson, with the possible exception of Sappho, the greatest woman poet of all time."

In the present edition all the poems of the preceding collections of poems are included in a single volume.

It has been erroneously assumed in a few instances that the chronological order in which Emily Dickinson's verse was written could be without much difficulty determined by the handwriting. Nothing could be further from the fact. The poems copied by the poet and included in letters to friends often had no relation to the actual time they were first written, as the first drafts sent to her Sister Sue reveal; while in her own tied packages of manuscript, arranged by herself, the order is arbitrary, even whimsical, and the period of the handwriting displayed is not necessarily the same as that of the original setting down. The long patient comparison of manuscript with manuscript, as well as their relation to letters and events and dates definitely noted by her family, will be obligatory to insure any credible sequence. And this remains the absorbing task of her editors.

Emily Dickinson Face to Face,[1] an expansion of the *Life and Letters,* was brought out in 1932. It is indispensable for the correction of ignorant and misleading conjecture, as well as for the more than one hundred and fifty letters and notes of the poet unavailable elsewhere. At the request of teachers and friends of young people the *Poems for Youth*[2] were selected and published, with many period illustrations, in 1934.

Emily Dickinson was primarily interested not in form but in what she had to say. Inevitably her verse form

[1] Houghton Mifflin Company.
[2] Little, Brown and Company.

has at times proved a stumbling block to some of her admirers. As her niece has said, "Metaphor is her characteristic figure and paradox her native tongue. No pedant could convict her of literary sin, nor yet convert her; and as long ago as 1860 Emily was outdating the imagists and writing free verse of her own invention. Her revolt was absolute; she abandoned rhyme altogether when she chose, and even assonance, writing in metre alone, like a Greek."[1] Nevertheless, Ludwig Lewisohn writes, "Her successes are many and varied and extraordinarily high. She can be of a compactness of expression and fullness of meaning not less than Goethean in Goethe's epigrammatic mood . . . She can add a new and heroic note to the eternal litany of love . . . She can soar like the intense mystical poets of the seventeenth century . . . And she can blend sobriety with vision and exactness with lyric lilt . . . And she can mock as Heine mocked and display the seamy side of the universe as seen by the optimists."[2] Louis Untermeyer calls her gnomic imagery "tremendous in implication", her quatrains "lavish with huge ideas and almost overpowering figures."[3]

The "summers of Hesperides" are long for Emily Dickinson. And still she is proving, by our mortal standards at least, that

> Eternity will be
> Velocity or pause,
> Precisely as the candidate
> Preliminary was.

A. L. H.

[1] *Poems of Emily Dickinson,* Centenary Edition.
[2] *Expression in America,* Harper & Brothers; pp. 359–360.
[3] *Modern American Poetry* (4th Revised Edition), Harcourt, Brace; p. 39.

No matter where
the Saints abide,
they make their
circuit fair
Behold how
great a
firmament
accompanies a Star.
—

ADDRESSED ON VERSO TO "SUSAN"

CONTENTS

PART ONE

LIFE

THIS is my letter to the world,
That never wrote to me, —
The simple news that Nature told,
With tender majesty.

Her message is committed
To hands I cannot see;
For love of her, sweet countrymen,
Judge tenderly of me!

· I ·

SUCCESS is counted sweetest
By those who ne'er succeed.
To comprehend a nectar
Requires sorest need.

Not one of all the purple host
Who took the flag to-day
Can tell the definition,
So clear, of victory,

As he, defeated, dying,
On whose forbidden ear
The distant strains of triumph
Break, agonized and clear.

· II ·

OUR share of night to bear,
Our share of morning,
Our blank in bliss to fill,
Our blank in scorning.

Here a star, and there a star,
Some lose their way.
Here a mist, and there a mist,
Afterwards — day!

· III ·

SOUL, wilt thou toss again?
By just such a hazard
Hundreds have lost, indeed,
But tens have won an all.

Angels' breathless ballot
Lingers to record thee;
Imps in eager caucus
Raffle for my soul.

· IV ·

'TIS so much joy! 'Tis so much joy!
If I should fail, what poverty!
And yet, as poor as I
Have ventured all upon a throw;
Have gained! Yes! Hesitated so
This side the victory!

Life is but life, and death but death!
Bliss is but bliss, and breath but breath!
And if, indeed, I fail,
At least to know the worst is sweet.
Defeat means nothing but defeat,
No drearier can prevail!

And if I gain, — oh, gun at sea,
Oh, bells that in the steeples be,
At first repeat it slow!
For heaven is a different thing
Conjectured, and waked sudden in,
And might o'erwhelm me so!

· V ·

GLEE! the great storm is over!
Four have recovered the land;
Forty gone down together
Into the boiling sand.

Ring, for the scant salvation!
Toll, for the bonnie souls, —
Neighbor and friend and bridegroom,
Spinning upon the shoals!

How they will tell the shipwreck
When winter shakes the door,
Till the children ask, "But the forty?
Did they come back no more?"

Then a silence suffuses the story,
And a softness the teller's eye;
And the children no further question,
And only the waves reply.

· VI ·

IF I can stop one heart from breaking,
I shall not live in vain;
If I can ease one life the aching,
Or cool one pain,
Or help one fainting robin
Unto his nest again,
I shall not live in vain.

· VII ·

WITHIN my reach!
I could have touched!
I might have chanced that way!
Soft sauntered through the village,
Sauntered as soft away!
So unsuspected violets
Within the fields lie low,
Too late for striving fingers
That passed, an hour ago.

· VIII ·

A WOUNDED deer leaps highest,
I've heard the hunter tell;
'Tis but the ecstasy of death,
And then the brake is still.

The smitten rock that gushes,
The trampled steel that springs:
A cheek is always redder
Just where the hectic stings!

Mirth is the mail of anguish,
In which it caution arm,
Lest anybody spy the blood
And "You're hurt" exclaim!

· IX ·

THE heart asks pleasure first,
And then, excuse from pain;
And then, those little anodynes
That deaden suffering;

And then, to go to sleep;
And then, if it should be
The will of its Inquisitor,
The liberty to die.

· X ·

A PRECIOUS, mouldering pleasure 'tis
To meet an antique book,
In just the dress his century wore;
A privilege, I think,

His venerable hand to take,
And warming in our own,
A passage back, or two, to make
To times when he was young.

His quaint opinions to inspect,
His knowledge to unfold
On what concerns our mutual mind,
The literature of old;

What interested scholars most,
What competitions ran
When Plato was a certainty,
And Sophocles a man;

When Sappho was a living girl,
And Beatrice wore
The gown that Dante deified.
Facts, centuries before,

He traverses familiar,
As one should come to town
And tell you all your dreams were true:
He lived where dreams were born.

His presence is enchantment,
You beg him not to go;
Old volumes shake their vellum heads
And tantalize, just so.

· XI ·

MUCH madness is divinest sense
To a discerning eye;
Much sense the starkest madness.

'Tis the majority
In this, as all, prevails.
Assent, and you are sane;
Demur, — you're straightway dangerous,
And handled with a chain.

·XII·

I ASKED no other thing,
No other was denied.
I offered Being for it;
The mighty merchant smiled.

Brazil? He twirled a button.
Without a glance my way:
"But, madam, is there nothing else
That we can show to-day?"

·XIII·

THE soul selects her own society,
Then shuts the door;
On her divine majority
Obtrude no more.

Unmoved, she notes the chariot's pausing
At her low gate;
Unmoved, an emperor is kneeling
Upon her mat.

I've known her from an ample nation
Choose one;
Then close the valves of her attention
Like stone.

· XIV ·

SOME things that fly there be, —
Birds, hours, the bumble-bee:
Of these no elegy.

Some things that stay there be, —
Grief, hills, eternity:
Nor this behooveth me.

There are, that resting, rise.
Can I expound the skies?
How still the riddle lies!

· XV ·

I KNOW some lonely houses off the road
A robber'd like the look of, —
Wooden barred,
And windows hanging low,
Inviting to
A portico,

Where two could creep:
One hand the tools,
The other peep
To make sure all's asleep.
Old-fashioned eyes,
Not easy to surprise!

How orderly the kitchen'd look by night,
With just a clock, —
But they could gag the tick,
And mice won't bark;
And so the walls don't tell,
None will.

A pair of spectacles ajar just stir —
An almanac's aware.
Was it the mat winked,
Or a nervous star?
The moon slides down the stair
To see who's there.

There's plunder, — where?
Tankard, or spoon,
Earring, or stone,
A watch, some ancient brooch
To match the grandmamma,
Staid sleeping there.

Day rattles, too,
Stealth's slow;
The sun has got as far
As the third sycamore.
Screams chanticleer,
"Who's there?"

And echoes, trains away,
Sneer — "Where?"
While the old couple, just astir,
Think that the sunrise left the door ajar!

· XVI ·

TO fight aloud is very brave,
But gallanter, I know,
Who charge within the bosom,
The cavalry of woe.

Who win, and nations do not see,
Who fall, and none observe,
Whose dying eyes no country
Regards with patriot love.

We trust, in plumed procession,
For such the angels go,
Rank after rank, with even feet
And uniforms of snow.

·XVII·

WHEN night is almost done,
And sunrise grows so near
That we can touch the spaces,
It's time to smooth the hair

And get the dimples ready,
And wonder we could care
For that old faded midnight
That frightened but an hour.

·XVIII·

READ, sweet, how others strove,
Till we are stouter;
What they renounced,
Till we are less afraid;
How many times they bore
The faithful witness,
Till we are helped,
As if a kingdom cared!

Read then of faith
That shone above the fagot;
Clear strains of hymn
The river could not drown;
Brave names of men
And celestial women,
Passed out of record
Into renown!

·XIX·

PAIN has an element of blank;
It cannot recollect
When it began, or if there were
A day when it was not.

It has no future but itself,
Its infinite realms contain
Its past, enlightened to perceive
New periods of pain.

·XX·

I TASTE a liquor never brewed,
From tankards scooped in pearl;
Not all the vats upon the Rhine
Yield such an alcohol!

Inebriate of air am I,
And debauchee of dew,
Reeling, through endless summer days,
From inns of molten blue.

When landlords turn the drunken bee
Out of the foxglove's door,
When butterflies renounce their drams,
I shall but drink the more!

Till seraphs swing their snowy hats,
And saints to windows run,
To see the little tippler
Leaning against the sun!

· XXI ·

HE ate and drank the precious words,
His spirit grew robust;
He knew no more that he was poor,
Nor that his frame was dust.
He danced along the dingy days,
And this bequest of wings
Was but a book. What liberty
A loosened spirit brings!

· XXII ·

I HAD no time to hate, because
The grave would hinder me,
And life was not so ample I
Could finish enmity.

Nor had I time to love; but since
Some industry must be,
The little toil of love, I thought,
Was large enough for me.

· XXIII ·

'TWAS such a little, little boat
That toddled down the bay!
'Twas such a gallant, gallant sea
That beckoned it away!

'Twas such a greedy, greedy wave
That licked it from the coast;
Nor ever guessed the stately sails
My little craft was lost!

· XXIV ·

WHETHER my bark went down at sea,
Whether she met with gales,
Whether to isles enchanted
She bent her docile sails;

By what mystic mooring
She is held to-day, —
This is the errand of the eye
Out upon the bay.

· XXV ·

BELSHAZZAR had a letter, —
He never had but one;
Belshazzar's correspondent
Concluded and begun
In that immortal copy
The conscience of us all
Can read without its glasses
On revelation's wall.

· XXVI ·

THE brain within its groove
Runs evenly and true;
But let a splinter swerve,
'Twere easier for you
To put the water back
When floods have slit the hills,
And scooped a turnpike for themselves,
And blotted out the mills!

·XXVII·

I'M nobody! Who are you?
Are you nobody, too?
Then there's a pair of us — don't tell!
They'd banish us, you know.

How dreary to be somebody!
How public, like a frog
To tell your name the livelong day
To an admiring bog!

·XXVIII·

I BRING an unaccustomed wine
To lips long parching, next to mine,
And summon them to drink.

Crackling with fever, they essay;
I turn my brimming eyes away,
And come next hour to look.

The hands still hug the tardy glass;
The lips I would have cooled, alas!
Are so superfluous cold,

I would as soon attempt to warm
The bosoms where the frost has lain
Ages beneath the mould.

Some other thirsty there may be
To whom this would have pointed me
Had it remained to speak.

And so I always bear the cup
If, haply, mine may be the drop
Some pilgrim thirst to slake, —

If, haply, any say to me,
"Unto the little, unto me,"
When I at last awake.

· XXIX ·

THE nearest dream recedes, unrealized.
The heaven we chase
Like the June bee
Before the school-boy
Invites the race,
Stoops to an easy clover —
Dips — evades — teases — deploys;
Then to the royal clouds
Lifts his light pinnace
Heedless of the boy
Staring, bewildered, at the mocking sky.

Homesick for steadfast honey,
Ah! the bee flies not
That brews that rare variety.

· XXX ·

WE play at paste,
Till qualified for pearl,
Then drop the paste,
And deem ourself a fool.
The shapes, though, were similar,
And our new hands
Learned gem-tactics
Practising sands.

·XXXI·

I FOUND the phrase to every thought
I ever had, but one;
And that defies me, — as a hand
Did try to chalk the sun

To races nurtured in the dark; —
How would your own begin?
Can blaze be done in cochineal,
Or noon in mazarin?

·XXXII·

HOPE is the thing with feathers
That perches in the soul,
And sings the tune without the words,
And never stops at all,

And sweetest in the gale is heard;
And sore must be the storm
That could abash the little bird
That kept so many warm.

I've heard it in the chillest land,
And on the strangest sea;
Yet, never, in extremity,
It asked a crumb of me.

·XXXIII·

DARE you see a soul at the white heat?
Then crouch within the door.
Red is the fire's common tint;
But when the vivid ore

Has sated flame's conditions,
 Its quivering substance plays
Without a color but the light
 Of unanointed blaze.

Least village boasts its blacksmith,
 Whose anvil's even din
Stands symbol for the finer forge
 That soundless tugs within,

Refining these impatient ores
 With hammer and with blaze,
Until the designated light
 Repudiate the forge.

· XXXIV ·

WHO never lost, are unprepared
A coronet to find;
Who never thirsted, flagons
And cooling tamarind.

Who never climbed the weary league —
Can such a foot explore
The purple territories
On Pizarro's shore?

How many legions overcome?
The emperor will say.
How many colors taken
On Revolution Day?

How many bullets bearest?
The royal scar hast thou?
Angels, write "Promoted"
On this soldier's brow!

·XXXV·

I CAN wade grief,
Whole pools of it, —
I'm used to that.
But the least push of joy
Breaks up my feet,
And I tip — drunken.
Let no pebble smile,
'Twas the new liquor, —
That was all!

Power is only pain,
Stranded, through discipline,
Till weights will hang.
Give balm to giants,
And they'll wilt, like men.
Give Himmaleh, —
They'll carry him!

·XXXVI·

I NEVER hear the word "escape"
Without a quicker blood,
A sudden expectation,
A flying attitude.

I never hear of prisons broad
By soldiers battered down,
But I tug childish at my bars, —
Only to fail again!

·XXXVII·

FOR each ecstatic instant
We must an anguish pay
In keen and quivering ratio
To the ecstasy.

For each beloved hour
Sharp pittances of years,
Bitter contested farthings
And coffers heaped with tears.

·XXXVIII·

THROUGH the straight pass of suffering
The martyrs even trod,
Their feet upon temptation,
Their faces upon God.

A stately, shriven company;
Convulsion playing round,
Harmless as streaks of meteor
Upon a planet's bound.

Their faith the everlasting troth;
Their expectation fair;
The needle to the north degree
Wades so, through polar air.

·XXXIX·

I MEANT to have but modest needs,
Such as content, and heaven;
Within my income these could lie,
And life and I keep even.

But since the last included both,
It would suffice my prayer
But just for one to stipulate,
And grace would grant the pair.

And so, upon this wise I prayed, —
Great Spirit, give to me
A heaven not so large as yours,
But large enough for me.

A smile suffused Jehovah's face;
The cherubim withdrew;
Grave saints stole out to look at me,
And showed their dimples, too.

I left the place with all my might, —
My prayer away I threw;
The quiet ages picked it up,
And Judgment twinkled, too,

That one so honest be extant
As take the tale for true
That "Whatsoever you shall ask,
Itself be given you."

But I, grown shrewder, scan the skies
With a suspicious air, —
As children, swindled for the first,
All swindlers be, infer.

·XL·

THE thought beneath so slight a film
Is more distinctly seen, —
As laces just reveal the surge,
Or mists the Apennine.

·XLI·

THE soul unto itself
Is an imperial friend, —
Or the most agonizing spy
An enemy could send.

Secure against its own,
No treason it can fear;
Itself its sovereign, of itself
The soul should stand in awe.

·XLII·

SURGEONS must be very careful
When they take the knife!
Underneath their fine incisions
Stirs the culprit, — Life!

·XLIII·

I LIKE to see it lap the miles,
And lick the valleys up,
And stop to feed itself at tanks;
And then, prodigious, step

Around a pile of mountains,
And, supercilious, peer
In shanties by the sides of roads;
And then a quarry pare

To fit its sides, and crawl between,
Complaining all the while
In horrid, hooting stanza;
Then chase itself down hill

And neigh like Boanerges;
Then, punctual as a star,
Stop — docile and omnipotent —
At its own stable door.

·XLIV·

THE show is not the show,
But they that go.
Menagerie to me
My neighbor be.
Fair play —
Both went to see.

·XLV·

DELIGHT becomes pictorial
When viewed through pain, —
More fair, because impossible
That any gain.

The mountain at a given distance
In amber lies;
Approached, the amber flits a little, —
And that's the skies!

·XLVI·

A THOUGHT went up my mind to-day
That I have had before,
But did not finish, — some way back,
I could not fix the year,

Nor where it went, nor why it came
The second time to me,
Nor definitely what it was,
Have I the art to say.

But somewhere in my soul, I know
I've met the thing before;
It just reminded me — 'twas all —
And came my way no more.

· XLVII ·

IS Heaven a physician?
They say that He can heal;
But medicine posthumous
Is unavailable.

Is Heaven an exchequer?
They speak of what we owe;
But that negotiation
I'm not a party to.

· XLVIII ·

THOUGH I get home how late, how late!
So I get home, 'twill compensate.
Better will be the ecstasy
That they have done expecting me,
When, night descending, dumb and dark,
They hear my unexpected knock.
Transporting must the moment be,
Brewed from decades of agony!

To think just how the fire will burn,
Just how long-cheated eyes will turn
To wonder what myself will say,
And what itself will say to me,
Beguiles the centuries of way!

· XLIX ·

A POOR torn heart, a tattered heart,
That sat it down to rest,
Nor noticed that the ebbing day
Flowed silver to the west,
Nor noticed night did soft descend
Nor constellation burn,
Intent upon the vision
Of latitudes unknown.

The angels, happening that way,
This dusty heart espied;
Tenderly took it up from toil
And carried it to God.
There, — sandals for the barefoot;
There, — gathered from the gales,
Do the blue havens by the hand
Lead the wandering sails.

· L ·

I SHOULD have been too glad, I see,
Too lifted for the scant degree
  Of life's penurious round;
My little circuit would have shamed
This new circumference, have blamed
  The homelier time behind.

I should have been too saved, I see,
Too rescued; fear too dim to me
  That I could spell the prayer
I knew so perfect yesterday, —
That scalding one, "Sabachthani",
  Recited fluent here.

Earth would have been too much, I see,
And heaven not enough for me;
  I should have had the joy
Without the fear to justify, —
The palm without the Calvary;
  So, Saviour, crucify.

Defeat whets victory, they say;
The reefs in old Gethsemane
  Endear the shore beyond.

'Tis beggars banquets best define;
'Tis thirsting vitalizes wine, —
Faith faints to understand.

·LI·

IT tossed and tossed, —
A little brig I knew, —
O'ertook by blast,
It spun and spun,
And groped delirious, for morn.

It slipped and slipped,
As one that drunken stepped;
Its white foot tripped,
Then dropped from sight.

Ah, brig, good-night
To crew and you;
The ocean's heart too smooth, too blue,
To break for you.

·LII·

VICTORY comes late,
And is held low to freezing lips
Too rapt with frost
To take it.

How sweet it would have tasted,
Just a drop!
Was God so economical?
His table's spread too high for us
Unless we dine on tip-toe.
Crumbs fit such little mouths,

Cherries suit robins;
The eagle's golden breakfast
Strangles them.
God keeps his oath to sparrows,
Who of little love
Know how to starve!

·LIII·

GOD gave a loaf to every bird,
But just a crumb to me;
I dare not eat it, though I starve, —
My poignant luxury
To own it, touch it, prove the feat
That made the pellet mine, —
Too happy in my sparrow chance
For ampler coveting.

It might be famine all around,
I could not miss an ear,
Such plenty smiles upon my board,
My garner shows so fair.
I wonder how the rich may feel, —
An Indiaman — an Earl?
I deem that I with but a crumb
Am sovereign of them all.

·LIV·

EXPERIMENT to me
Is every one I meet.
If it contain a kernel?
The figure of a nut

Presents upon a tree,
Equally plausibly;
But meat within is requisite,
To squirrels and to me.

·LV·

MY country need not change her gown,
Her triple suit as sweet
As when 'twas cut at Lexington,
And first pronounced "a fit."

Great Britain disapproves "the stars";
Disparagement discreet, —
There's something in their attitude
That taunts her bayonet.

·LVI·

FAITH is a fine invention
For gentlemen who see;
But microscopes are prudent
In an emergency!

·LVII·

EXCEPT the heaven had come so near,
So seemed to choose my door,
The distance would not haunt me so;
I had not hoped before.

But just to hear the grace depart
I never thought to see,
Afflicts me with a double loss;
'Tis lost, and lost to me.

·LVIII·

PORTRAITS are to daily faces
As an evening west
To a fine, pedantic sunshine
In a satin vest.

·LIX·

I TOOK my power in my hand
And went against the world;
'Twas not so much as David had,
But I was twice as bold.

I aimed my pebble, but myself
Was all the one that fell.
Was it Goliath was too large,
Or only I too small?

·LX·

A SHADY friend for torrid days
Is easier to find
Than one of higher temperature
For frigid hour of mind.

The vane a little to the east
Scares muslin souls away;
If broadcloth breasts are firmer
Than those of organdy,

Who is to blame? The weaver?
Ah! the bewildering thread!
The tapestries of paradise
So notelessly are made!

·LXI·

EACH life converges to some centre
Expressed or still;
Exists in every human nature
A goal,

Admitted scarcely to itself, it may be,
Too fair
For credibility's temerity
To dare.

Adored with caution, as a brittle heaven,
To reach
Were hopeless as the rainbow's raiment
To touch,

Yet persevered toward, surer for the distance;
How high
Unto the saints' slow diligence
The sky!

Ungained, it may be, by life's low venture,
But then,
Eternity enables the endeavoring
Again.

·LXII·

BEFORE I got my eye put out,
I liked as well to see
As other creatures that have eyes,
And know no other way.

But were it told to me, to-day,
That I might have the sky
For mine, I tell you that my heart
Would split, for size of me.

The meadows mine, the mountains mine, —
All forests, stintless stars,
As much of noon as I could take
Between my finite eyes.

The motions of the dipping birds,
The lightning's jointed road,
For mine to look at when I liked, —
The news would strike me dead!

So, safer, guess, with just my soul
Upon the window-pane
Where other creatures put their eyes,
Incautious of the sun.

·LXIII·

TALK with prudence to a beggar
Of "Potosi" and the mines!
Reverently to the hungry
Of your viands and your wines!

Cautious, hint to any captive
You have passed enfranchised feet!
Anecdotes of air in dungeons
Have sometimes proved deadly sweet!

·LXIV·

HE preached upon "breadth" till it argued him narrow, —
The broad are too broad to define;
And of "truth" until it proclaimed him a liar, —
The truth never flaunted a sign.

Simplicity fled from his counterfeit presence
As gold the pyrites would shun.
What confusion would cover the innocent Jesus
To meet so enabled a man!

·LXV·

GOOD night! which put the candle out?
A jealous zephyr, not a doubt.
Ah! friend, you little knew
How long at that celestial wick
The angels labored diligent;
Extinguished, now, for you!

It might have been the lighthouse spark
Some sailor, rowing in the dark,
Had importuned to see!
It might have been the waning lamp
That lit the drummer from the camp
To purer reveille!

·LXVI·

WHEN I hoped I feared,
Since I hoped I dared;
Everywhere alone
As a church remain;
Spectre cannot harm,
Serpent cannot charm;
He deposes doom,
Who hath suffered him.

·LXVII·

A DEED knocks first at thought,
And then it knocks at will.
That is the manufacturing spot,
And will at home and well.

It then goes out an act,
Or is entombed so still
That only to the ear of God
Its doom is audible.

LXVIII·

MINE enemy is growing old, —
I have at last revenge.
The palate of the hate departs;
If any would avenge, —

Let him be quick, the viand flits,
It is a faded meat.
Anger as soon as fed is dead;
'Tis starving makes it fat.

·LXIX·

REMORSE is memory awake,
Her companies astir, —
A presence of departed acts
At window and at door.

Its past set down before the soul,
And lighted with a match,
Perusal to facilitate
Of its condensed despatch.

Remorse is cureless, — the disease
Not even God can heal;
For 'tis His institution, —
The complement of hell.

·LXX·

THE body grows outside, —
The more convenient way, —
That if the spirit like to hide,
Its temple stands alway

Ajar, secure, inviting;
It never did betray
The soul that asked its shelter
In timid honesty.

·LXXI·

UNDUE significance a starving man attaches
To food
Far off; he sighs, and therefore hopeless,
And therefore good.

Partaken, it relieves indeed, but proves us
That spices fly
In the receipt. It was the distance
Was savory.

·LXXII·

HEART not so heavy as mine,
Wending late home,
As it passed my window
Whistled itself a tune, —

A careless snatch, a ballad,
A ditty of the street;
Yet to my irritated ear
An anodyne so sweet,

It was as if a bobolink,
Sauntering this way,
Carolled and mused and carolled,
Then bubbled slow away.

It was as if a chirping brook
Upon a toilsome way
Set bleeding feet to minuets
Without the knowing why.

To-morrow, night will come again,
Weary, perhaps, and sore.
Ah, bugle, by my window,
I pray you stroll once more!

·LXXIII·

I MANY times thought peace had come,
When peace was far away;
As wrecked men deem they sight the land
At centre of the sea,

And struggle slacker, but to prove,
As hopelessly as I,
How many the fictitious shores
Before the harbor lie.

·LXXIV·

UNTO my books so good to turn
Far ends of tired days;
It half endears the abstinence,
And pain is missed in praise.

As flavors cheer retarded guests
With banquetings to be,
So spices stimulate the time
Till my small library.

It may be wilderness without,
Far feet of failing men,
But holiday excludes the night,
And it is bells within.

I thank these kinsmen of the shelf;
Their countenances bland
Enamour in prospective,
And satisfy, obtained.

·LXXV·

THIS merit hath the worst, —
It cannot be again.
When Fate hath taunted last
And thrown her furthest stone,

The maimed may pause and breathe,
And glance securely round.
The deer invites no longer
Than it eludes the hound.

·LXXVI·

I HAD been hungry all the years;
My noon had come, to dine;
I, trembling, drew the table near,
And touched the curious wine.

'Twas this on tables I had seen,
When turning, hungry, lone,
I looked in windows, for the wealth
I could not hope to own.

I did not know the ample bread,
'Twas so unlike the crumb
The birds and I had often shared
In Nature's dining-room.

The plenty hurt me, 'twas so new, —
Myself felt ill and odd,
As berry of a mountain bush
Transplanted to the road.

Nor was I hungry; so I found
That hunger was a way
Of persons outside windows,
The entering takes away.

·LXXVII·

I GAINED it so,
By climbing slow,
By catching at the twigs that grow
Between the bliss and me.
It hung so high,
As well the sky
Attempt by strategy.

I said I gained it, —
This was all.
Look, how I clutch it,
Lest it fall,
And I a pauper go;
Unfitted by an instant's grace
For the contented beggar's face
I wore an hour ago.

·LXXVIII·

TO learn the transport by the pain,
As blind men learn the sun;
To die of thirst, suspecting
That brooks in meadows run;

To stay the homesick, homesick feet
Upon a foreign shore
Haunted by native lands, the while,
And blue, beloved air —

This is the sovereign anguish,
This, the signal woe!
These are the patient laureates
Whose voices, trained below,

Ascend in ceaseless carol,
Inaudible, indeed,
To us, the duller scholars
Of the mysterious bard!

·LXXIX·

I YEARS had been from home,
And now, before the door,
I dared not open, lest a face
I never saw before

Stare vacant into mine
And ask my business there.
My business, — just a life I left,
Was such still dwelling there?

I fumbled at my nerve,
I scanned the windows near;
The silence like an ocean rolled,
And broke against my ear.

I laughed a wooden laugh
That I could fear a door,
Who danger and the dead had faced,
But never quaked before.

I fitted to the latch
My hand, with trembling care,
Lest back the awful door should spring,
And leave me standing there.

I moved my fingers off
As cautiously as glass,
And held my ears, and like a thief
Fled gasping from the house.

· L X X X ·

PRAYER is the little implement
Through which men reach
Where presence is denied them.
They fling their speech

By means of it in God's ear;
If then He hear,
This sums the apparatus
Comprised in prayer.

· L X X X I ·

I KNOW that he exists
Somewhere, in silence.
He has hid his rare life
From our gross eyes.

'Tis in instant's play,
'Tis a fond ambush,
Just to make bliss
Earn her own surprise!

But should the play
Prove piercing earnest,
Should the glee glaze
In death's stiff stare,

Would not the fun
Look too expensive?
Would not the jest
Have crawled too far?

·LXXXII·

MUSICIANS wrestle everywhere:
All day, among the crowded air,
  I hear the silver strife;
And — waking long before the dawn —
Such transport breaks upon the town
  I think it that "new life!"

It is not bird, it has no nest;
Nor band, in brass and scarlet dressed,
  Nor tambourine, nor man;
It is not hymn from pulpit read, —
The morning stars the treble led
  On time's first afternoon!

Some say it is the spheres at play!
Some say that bright majority
  Of vanished dames and men!
Some think it service in the place
Where we, with late, celestial face,
  Please God, shall ascertain!

·LXXXIII·

JUST lost when I was saved!
Just felt the world go by!
Just girt me for the onset with eternity,
When breath blew back,
And on the other side
I heard recede the disappointed tide!

Therefore, as one returned, I feel,
Odd secrets of the line to tell!
Some sailor, skirting foreign shores,
Some pale reporter from the awful doors
Before the seal!

Next time, to stay!
Next time, the things to see
By ear unheard,
Unscrutinized by eye.

Next time, to tarry,
While the ages steal, —
Slow tramp the centuries,
And the cycles wheel.

· LXXXIV ·

'TIS little I could care for pearls
Who own the ample sea;
Or brooches, when the Emperor
With rubies pelteth me;

Or gold, who am the Prince of Mines;
Or diamonds, when I see
A diadem to fit a dome
Continual crowning me.

· LXXXV ·

SUPERIORITY to fate
Is difficult to learn.
'Tis not conferred by any,
But possible to earn

A pittance at a time,
Until, to her surprise,
The soul with strict economy
Subsists till Paradise.

·LXXXVI·

HOPE is a subtle glutton;
He feeds upon the fair;
And yet, inspected closely,
What abstinence is there!

His is the halcyon table
That never seats but one,
And whatsoever is consumed
The same amounts remain.

·LXXXVII·

FORBIDDEN fruit a flavor has
That lawful orchards mocks;
How luscious lies the pea within
The pod that Duty locks!

·LXXXVIII·

HEAVEN is what I cannot reach!
The apple on the tree,
Provided it do hopeless hang,
That "heaven" is, to me.

The color on the cruising cloud,
The interdicted ground
Behind the hill, the house behind, —
There Paradise is found!

·LXXXIX·

A WORD is dead
When it is said,
Some say.
I say it just
Begins to live
That day.

· X C ·

TO venerate the simple days
  Which lead the seasons by,
Needs but to remember
  That from you or me
They may take the trifle
  Termed mortality!

To invest existence with a stately air,
Needs but to remember
  That the acorn there
Is the egg of forests
  For the upper air!

· X C I ·

IT'S such a little thing to weep,
  So short a thing to sigh;
And yet by trades the size of these
  We men and women die!

· X C I I ·

DROWNING is not so pitiful
  As the attempt to rise.
Three times, 'tis said, a sinking man
  Comes up to face the skies,
And then declines forever
  To that abhorred abode

Where hope and he part company, —
  For he is grasped of God.
The Maker's cordial visage,
  However good to see,
Is shunned, we must admit it,
  Like an adversity.

· XCIII ·

HOW still the bells in steeples stand,
  Till, swollen with the sky,
They leap upon their silver feet
  In frantic melody!

· XCIV ·

IF the foolish call them "flowers",
  Need the wiser tell?
If the savants "classify" them,
  It is just as well!

Those who read the *Revelations*
  Must not criticise
Those who read the same edition
  With beclouded eyes!

Could we stand with that old Moses
  Canaan denied, —
Scan, like him, the stately landscape
  On the other side, —

Doubtless we should deem superfluous
  Many sciences
Not pursued by learnèd angels
  In scholastic skies!

Low amid that glad *Belles lettres*
  Grant that we may stand,
Stars, amid profound Galaxies,
  At that grand "Right hand"!

· XCV ·

COULD any mortal lip divine
  The undeveloped freight
Of a delivered syllable,
  'Twould crumble with the weight.

· XCVI ·

MY life closed twice before its close;
  It yet remains to see
If Immortality unveil
  A third event to me,

So huge, so hopeless to conceive,
  As these that twice befell.
Parting is all we know of heaven,
  And all we need of hell.

· XCVII ·

WE never know how high we are
  Till we are called to rise;
And then, if we are true to plan,
  Our statures touch the skies.

The heroism we recite
  Would be a daily thing,
Did not ourselves the cubits warp
  For fear to be a king.

· XCVIII ·

WHILE I was fearing it, it came,
  But came with less of fear,
Because that fearing it so long
  Had almost made it dear.
There is a fitting a dismay,
  A fitting a despair.

'Tis harder knowing it is due,
  Than knowing it is here.
The trying on the utmost,
  The morning it is new,
Is terribler than wearing it
  A whole existence through.

· XCIX ·

THERE is no frigate like a book
  To take us lands away,
Nor any coursers like a page
  Of prancing poetry.

This traverse may the poorest take
  Without oppress of toll;
How frugal is the chariot
  That bears a human soul!

· C ·

WHO has not found the heaven below
  Will fail of it above.
God's residence is next to mine,
  His furniture is love.

· CI ·

A FACE devoid of love or grace,
A hateful, hard, successful face,
  A face with which a stone
Would feel as thoroughly at ease
As were they old acquaintances, —
  First time together thrown.

·CII·

I HAD a guinea golden;
I lost it in the sand,
And though the sum was simple,
And pounds were in the land,
Still had it such a value
Unto my frugal eye,
That when I could not find it
I sat me down to sigh.

I had a crimson robin
Who sang full many a day,
But when the woods were painted
He, too, did fly away.
Time brought me other robins, —
Their ballads were the same, —
Still for my missing troubadour
I kept the "house at hame."

I had a star in heaven;
One Pleiad was its name,
And when I was not heeding
It wandered from the same.
And though the skies are crowded,
And all the night ashine,
I do not care about it,
Since none of them are mine.

My story has a moral:
I have a missing friend, —
Pleiad its name, and robin,
And guinea in the sand, —
And when this mournful ditty,
Accompanied with tear,
Shall meet the eye of traitor

In country far from here,
Grant that repentance solemn
May seize upon his mind,
And he no consolation
Beneath the sun may find.

·CIII·

FROM all the jails the boys and girls
Ecstatically leap, —
Beloved, only afternoon
That prison doesn't keep.

They storm the earth and stun the air,
A mob of solid bliss.
Alas! that frowns could lie in wait
For such a foe as this!

·CIV·

FEW get enough, — enough is one,
To that ethereal throng
Have not each one of us the right
To stealthily belong?

·CV·

UPON the gallows hung a wretch,
Too sullied for the hell
To which the law entitled him.
As nature's curtain fell
The one who bore him tottered in,
For this was woman's son.
"'Twas all I had," she stricken gasped;
Oh, what a livid boon!

· CVI ·

I FELT a cleavage in my mind
As if my brain had split;
I tried to match it, seam by seam,
But could not make them fit.

The thought behind I strove to join
Unto the thought before,
But sequence ravelled out of reach
Like balls upon a floor.

· CVII ·

THE reticent volcano keeps
His never slumbering plan;
Confided are his projects pink
To no precarious man.

If nature will not tell the tale
Jehovah told to her,
Can human nature not survive
Without a listener?

Admonished by her buckled lips
Let every babbler be.
The only secret people keep
Is Immortality.

· CVIII ·

IF recollecting were forgetting,
Then I remember not;
And if forgetting, recollecting,
How near I had forgot!
And if to miss were merry,
And if to mourn were gay,
How very blithe the fingers
That gathered these to-day!

· CIX ·

THE farthest thunder that I heard
Was nearer than the sky,
And rumbles still, though torrid noons
Have lain their missiles by.
The lightning that preceded it
Struck no one but myself,
But I would not exchange the bolt
For all the rest of life.
Indebtedness to oxygen
The chemist may repay,
But not the obligation
To electricity.
It founds the homes and decks the days,
And every clamor bright
Is but the gleam concomitant
Of that waylaying light.
The thought is quiet as a flake, —
A crash without a sound;
How life's reverberation
Its explanation found!

· CX ·

ON the bleakness of my lot
Bloom I strove to raise.
Late, my acre of a rock
Yielded grape and maize.

Soil of flint if steadfast tilled
Will reward the hand;
Seed of palm by Lybian sun
Fructified in sand.

· CXI ·

A DOOR just opened on a street —
I, lost, was passing by —
An instant's width of warmth disclosed,
And wealth, and company.

The door as sudden shut, and I,
I, lost, was passing by, —
Lost doubly, but by contrast most,
Enlightening misery.

· CXII ·

ARE friends delight or pain?
Could bounty but remain
Riches were good.

But if they only stay
Bolder to fly away,
Riches are sad.

· CXIII ·

ASHES denote that fire was;
Respect the grayest pile
For the departed creature's sake
That hovered there awhile.

Fire exists the first in light,
And then consolidates, —
Only the chemist can disclose
Into what carbonates.

· CXIV ·

FATE slew him, but he did not drop;
She felled — he did not fall —
Impaled him on her fiercest stakes —
He neutralized them all.

She stung him, sapped his firm advance,
But, when her worst was done,
And he, unmoved, regarded her,
Acknowledged him a man.

·CXV·

FINITE to fail, but infinite to venture.
For the one ship that struts the shore
Many's the gallant, overwhelmed creature
Nodding in navies nevermore.

·CXVI·

I MEASURE every grief I meet
With analytic eyes;
I wonder if it weighs like mine,
Or has an easier size.

I wonder if they bore it long,
Or did it just begin?
I could not tell the date of mine,
It feels so old a pain.

I wonder if it hurts to live,
And if they have to try,
And whether, could they choose between,
They would not rather die.

I wonder if when years have piled —
Some thousands — on the cause
Of early hurt, if such a lapse
Could give them any pause;

Or would they go on aching still
Through centuries above,
Enlightened to a larger pain
By contrast with the love.

The grieved are many, I am told;
  The reason deeper lies, —
Death is but one and comes but once,
  And only nails the eyes.

There's grief of want, and grief of cold, —
  A sort they call "despair";
There's banishment from native eyes,
  In sight of native air.

And though I may not guess the kind
  Correctly, yet to me
A piercing comfort it affords
  In passing Calvary,

To note the fashions of the cross,
  Of those that stand alone,
Still fascinated to presume
  That some are like my own.

·CXVII·

I HAVE a king who does not speak;
So, wondering, thro' the hours meek
  I trudge the day away, —
Half glad when it is night and sleep,
If, haply, thro' a dream to peep
  In parlors shut by day.

And if I do, when morning comes,
It is as if a hundred drums
  Did round my pillow roll,
And shouts fill all my childish sky,
And bells keep saying "victory"
  From steeples in my soul!

And if I don't, the little Bird
Within the Orchard is not heard,
And I omit to pray,
"Father, thy will be done" to-day,
For my will goes the other way,
And it were perjury!

· CXVIII ·

IT dropped so low in my regard
I heard it hit the ground,
And go to pieces on the stones
At bottom of my mind;

Yet blamed the fate that fractured, less
Than I reviled myself
For entertaining plated wares
Upon my silver shelf.

· CXIX ·

TO lose one's faith surpasses
The loss of an estate,
Because estates can be
Replenished, — faith cannot.

Inherited with life,
Belief but once can be;
Annihilate a single clause,
And Being's beggary.

· CXX ·

I HAD a daily bliss
I half indifferent viewed,
Till sudden I perceived it stir, —
It grew as I pursued,

Till when, around a crag,
It wasted from my sight,
Enlarged beyond my utmost scope,
I learned its sweetness right.

·CXXI·

I WORKED for chaff, and earning wheat
Was haughty and betrayed.
What right had fields to arbitrate
In matters ratified?

I tasted wheat, — and hated chaff,
And thanked the ample friend;
Wisdom is more becoming viewed
At distance than at hand.

·CXXII·

LIFE, and Death, and Giants
Such as these, are still.
Minor apparatus, hopper of the mill,
Beetle at the candle,
Or a fife's small fame,
Maintain by accident
That they proclaim.

·CXXIII·

OUR lives are Swiss, —
So still, so cool,
Till, some odd afternoon,
The Alps neglect their curtains,
And we look farther on.

Italy stands the other side,
While, like a guard between,
The solemn Alps,
The siren Alps,
Forever intervene!

·CXXIV·

REMEMBRANCE has a rear and front, —
'Tis something like a house;
It has a garret also
For refuge and the mouse,

Besides, the deepest cellar
That ever mason hewed;
Look to it, by its fathoms
Ourselves be not pursued.

·CXXV·

TO hang our head ostensibly,
And subsequent to find
That such was not the posture
Of our immortal mind,

Affords the sly presumption
That, in so dense a fuzz,
You, too, take cobweb attitudes
Upon a plane of gauze!

·CXXVI·

THE brain is wider than the sky,
For, put them side by side,
The one the other will include
With ease, and you beside.

The brain is deeper than the sea,
For, hold them, blue to blue,
The one the other will absorb,
As sponges, buckets do.

The brain is just the weight of God,
For, lift them, pound for pound,
And they will differ, if they do,
As syllable from sound.

·CXXVII·

THE bone that has no marrow;
What ultimate for that?
It is not fit for table,
For beggar, or for cat.

A bone has obligations,
A being has the same;
A marrowless assembly
Is culpabler than shame.

But how shall finished creatures
A function fresh obtain? —
Old Nicodemus' phantom
Confronting us again!

·CXXVIII·

THE past is such a curious creature,
To look her in the face
A transport may reward us,
Or a disgrace.

Unarmed if any meet her,
I charge him, fly!
Her rusty ammunition
Might yet reply!

·CXXIX·

TO help our bleaker parts
Salubrious hours are given,
Which if they do not fit for earth
Drill silently for heaven.

·CXXX·

WHAT soft, cherubic creatures
These gentlewomen are!
One would as soon assault a plush
Or violate a star.

Such dimity convictions,
A horror so refined
Of freckled human nature,
Of Deity ashamed, —

It's such a common glory,
A fisherman's degree!
Redemption, brittle lady,
Be so ashamed of thee.

·CXXXI·

WHO never wanted, — maddest joy
Remains to him unknown;
The banquet of abstemiousness
Surpasses that of wine.

Within its hope, though yet ungrasped
Desire's perfect goal,
No nearer, lest reality
Should disenthrall thy soul.

·CXXXII·

IT might be easier
To fail with land in sight,
Than gain my blue peninsula
To perish of delight.

·CXXXIII·

YOU cannot put a fire out;
A thing that can ignite
Can go, itself, without a fan
Upon the slowest night.

You cannot fold a flood
And put it in a drawer, —
Because the winds would find it out,
And tell your cedar floor.

·CXXXIV·

A MODEST lot, a fame *petite,*
A brief campaign of sting and sweet
Is plenty! Is enough!
A sailor's business is the shore,
A soldier's — balls. Who asketh more
Must seek the neighboring life!

·CXXXV·

IS bliss, then, such abyss
I must not put my foot amiss
For fear I spoil my shoe?

I'd rather suit my foot
Than save my boot,
For yet to buy another pair
Is possible
At any fair.

But bliss is sold just once;
The patent lost
None buy it any more.

·CXXXVI·

I STEPPED from plank to plank
So slow and cautiously;
The stars about my head I felt,
About my feet the sea.

I knew not but the next
Would be my final inch, —
This gave me that precarious gait
Some call experience.

·CXXXVII·

ONE day is there of the series
Termed Thanksgiving day,
Celebrated part at table,
Part in memory.

Neither patriarch nor pussy,
I dissect the play;
Seems it, to my hooded thinking,
Reflex holiday.

Had there been no sharp subtraction
From the early sum,
Not an acre or a caption
Where was once a room,

Not a mention, whose small pebble
Wrinkled any bay, —
Unto such, were such assembly,
'Twere Thanksgiving day.

· CXXXVIII ·

SOFTENED by Time's consummate plush,
How sleek the woe appears
That threatened childhood's citadel
And undermined the years!

Bisected now by bleaker griefs,
We envy the despair
That devastated childhood's realm,
So easy to repair.

PART TWO

NATURE

My nosegays are for captives;
Dim, long-expectant eyes,
Fingers denied the plucking,
Patient till paradise.

To such, if they should whisper
Of morning and the moor,
They bear no other errand,
And I, no other prayer.

· I ·

NATURE, the gentlest mother,
Impatient of no child,
The feeblest or the waywardest, —
Her admonition mild

In forest and the hill
By traveller is heard,
Restraining rampant squirrel
Or too impetuous bird.

How fair her conversation,
A summer afternoon, —
Her household, her assembly;
And when the sun goes down

Her voice among the aisles
Incites the timid prayer
Of the minutest cricket,
The most unworthy flower.

When all the children sleep
She turns as long away
As will suffice to light her lamps;
Then, bending from the sky,

With infinite affection
And infiniter care,
Her golden finger on her lip,
Wills silence everywhere.

· II ·

WILL there really be a morning?
Is there such a thing as day?
Could I see it from the mountains
If I were as tall as they?

Has it feet like water-lilies?
Has it feathers like a bird?
Is it brought from famous countries
Of which I have never heard?

Oh, some scholar! Oh, some sailor!
Oh, some wise man from the skies!
Please to tell a little pilgrim
Where the place called morning lies!

·III·

AT half-past three a single bird
Unto a silent sky
Propounded but a single term
Of cautious melody.

At half-past four, experiment
Had subjugated test,
And lo! her silver principle
Supplanted all the rest.

At half-past seven, element
Nor implement was seen,
And place was where the presence was,
Circumference between.

·IV·

THE day came slow, till five o'clock,
Then sprang before the hills
Like hindered rubies, or the light
A sudden musket spills.

The purple could not keep the east,
The sunrise shook from fold,
Like breadths of topaz, packed a night,
The lady just unrolled.

The happy winds their timbrels took;
The birds, in docile rows,
Arranged themselves around their prince —
(The wind is prince of those).

The orchard sparkled like a Jew, —
How mighty 'twas, to stay
A guest in this stupendous place,
The parlor of the day!

· V ·

THE sun just touched the morning;
The morning, happy thing,
Supposed that he had come to dwell,
And life would be all spring.

She felt herself supremer, —
A raised, ethereal thing;
Henceforth for her what holiday!
Meanwhile, her wheeling king

Trailed slow along the orchards
His haughty, spangled hems,
Leaving a new necessity, —
The want of diadems!

The morning fluttered, staggered,
Felt feebly for her crown, —
Her unanointed forehead
Henceforth her only one.

· VI ·

THE robin is the one
That interrupts the morn
With hurried, few, express reports
When March is scarcely on.

The robin is the one
That overflows the noon
With her cherubic quantity,
An April but begun.

The robin is the one
That speechless from her nest
Submits that home and certainty
And sanctity are best.

· VII ·

FROM cocoon forth a butterfly
As lady from her door
Emerged — a summer afternoon —
Repairing everywhere,

Without design, that I could trace,
Except to stray abroad
On miscellaneous enterprise
The clovers understood.

Her pretty parasol was seen
Contracting in a field
Where men made hay, then struggling hard
With an opposing cloud,

Where parties, phantom as herself,
To Nowhere seemed to go
In purposeless circumference,
As 'twere a tropic show.

And notwithstanding bee that worked,
And flower that zealous blew,
This audience of idleness
Disdained them, from the sky,

Till sundown crept, a steady tide,
And men that made the hay,
And afternoon, and butterfly,
Extinguished in its sea.

·VIII·

BEFORE you thought of spring,
Except as a surmise,
You see, God bless his suddenness,
A fellow in the skies
Of independent hues,
A little weather-worn,
Inspiriting habiliments
Of indigo and brown.

With specimens of song,
As if for you to choose,
Discretion in the interval,
With gay delays he goes
To some superior tree
Without a single leaf,
And shouts for joy to nobody
But his seraphic self!

·IX·

AN altered look about the hills;
A Tyrian light the village fills;
A wider sunrise in the dawn;
A deeper twilight on the lawn;
A print of a vermilion foot;
A purple finger on the slope;
A flippant fly upon the pane;
A spider at his trade again;

An added strut in chanticleer;
A flower expected everywhere;
An axe shrill singing in the woods;
Fern-odors on untravelled roads, —
All this, and more I cannot tell,
A furtive look you know as well,
And Nicodemus' mystery
Receives its annual reply.

· X ·

"WHOSE are the little beds," I asked,
"Which in the valleys lie?"
Some shook their heads, and others smiled,
And no one made reply.

"Perhaps they did not hear," I said;
"I will inquire again.
Whose are the beds, the tiny beds
So thick upon the plain?"

" 'Tis daisy in the shortest;
A little farther on,
Nearest the door to wake the first,
Little leontodon.

" 'Tis iris, sir, and aster,
Anemone and bell,
Batschia in the blanket red,
And chubby daffodil."

Meanwhile at many cradles
Her busy foot she plied,
Humming the quaintest lullaby
That ever rocked a child.

"Hush! Epigea wakens!
The crocus stirs her lids,
Rhodora's cheek is crimson, —
She's dreaming of the woods."

Then, turning from them, reverent,
"Their bed-time 'tis," she said;
"The bumble-bees will wake them
When April woods are red."

· XI ·

PIGMY seraphs gone astray,
Velvet people from Vevay,
Belles from some lost summer day,
Bees' exclusive coterie.
Paris could not lay the fold
Belted down with emerald;
Venice could not show a cheek
Of a tint so lustrous meek.
Never such an ambuscade
As of brier and leaf displayed
For my little damask maid.
I had rather wear her grace
Than an earl's distinguished face;

I had rather dwell like her
Than be Duke of Exeter,
Royalty enough for me
To subdue the bumble-bee!

· XII ·

TO hear an oriole sing
May be a common thing,
Or only a divine.

It is not of the bird
Who sings the same, unheard,
As unto crowd.

The fashion of the ear
Attireth that it hear
In dun or fair.

So whether it be rune,
Or whether it be none,
Is of within;

The "tune is in the tree,"
The sceptic showeth me;
"No, sir! In thee!"

· XIII ·

ONE of the ones that Midas touched,
Who failed to touch us all,
Was that confiding prodigal,
The blissful oriole.

So drunk, he disavows it
With badinage divine;
So dazzling, we mistake him
For an alighting mine.

A pleader, a dissembler,
An epicure, a thief, —
Betimes an oratorio,
An ecstasy in chief;

The Jesuit of orchards,
He cheats as he enchants
Of an entire attar
For his decamping wants.

The splendor of a Burmah,
The meteor of birds,
Departing like a pageant
Of ballads and of bards.

I never thought that Jason sought
For any golden fleece;
But then I am a rural man,
With thoughts that make for peace.

But if there were a Jason,
Tradition suffer me
Behold his lost emolument
Upon the apple-tree.

· XIV ·

I DREADED that first robin so,
But he is mastered now,
And I'm accustomed to him grown, —
He hurts a little, though.

I thought if I could only live
Till that first shout got by,
Not all pianos in the woods
Had power to mangle me.

I dared not meet the daffodils,
For fear their yellow gown
Would pierce me with a fashion
So foreign to my own.

I wished the grass would hurry,
So when 'twas time to see,
He'd be too tall, the tallest one
Could stretch to look at me.

I could not bear the bees should come,
I wished they'd stay away
In those dim countries where they go:
What word had they for me?

They're here, though; not a creature failed,
No blossom stayed away
In gentle deference to me,
The Queen of Calvary.

Each one salutes me as he goes,
And I my childish plumes
Lift, in bereaved acknowledgment
Of their unthinking drums.

· XV ·

A ROUTE of evanescence
With a revolving wheel;
A resonance of emerald,
A rush of cochineal;
And every blossom on the bush
Adjusts its tumbled head, —
The mail from Tunis, probably,
An easy morning's ride.

· XVI ·

THE skies can't keep their secret!
They tell it to the hills —
The hills just tell the orchards —
And they the daffodils!

A bird, by chance, that goes that way
Soft overheard the whole.
If I should bribe the little bird,
Who knows but she would tell?

I think I won't, however,
It's finer not to know;
If summer were an axiom,
What sorcery had snow?

So keep your secret, Father!
I would not, if I could,
Know what the sapphire fellows do,
In your new-fashioned world!

·XVII·

WHO robbed the woods,
The trusting woods?
The unsuspecting trees
Brought out their burrs and mosses
His fantasy to please.
He scanned their trinkets, curious,
He grasped, he bore away.
What will the solemn hemlock,
What will the fir-tree say?

·XVIII·

TWO butterflies went out at noon
And waltzed above a stream,
Then stepped straight through the firmament
And rested on a beam;

And then together bore away
Upon a shining sea, —
Though never yet, in any port,
Their coming mentioned be.

If spoken by the distant bird,
If met in ether sea
By frigate or by merchantman,
Report was not to me.

· XIX ·

I STARTED early, took my dog,
And visited the sea;
The mermaids in the basement
Came out to look at me,

And frigates in the upper floor
Extended hempen hands,
Presuming me to be a mouse
Aground, upon the sands.

But no man moved me till the tide
Went past my simple shoe,
And past my apron and my belt,
And past my bodice too,

And made as he would eat me up
As wholly as a dew
Upon a dandelion's sleeve —
And then I started too.

And he — he followed close behind;
I felt his silver heel
Upon my ankle, — then my shoes
Would overflow with pearl.

Until we met the solid town,
No man he seemed to know;
And bowing with a mighty look
At me, the sea withdrew.

· XX ·

ARCTURUS is his other name, —
I'd rather call him star!
It's so unkind of science
To go and interfere!

I pull a flower from the woods, —
A monster with a glass
Computes the stamens in a breath,
And has her in a class.

Whereas I took the butterfly
Aforetime in my hat,
He sits erect in cabinets,
The clover-bells forgot.

What once was heaven, is zenith now.
Where I proposed to go
When time's brief masquerade was done,
Is mapped, and charted too!

What if the poles should frisk about
And stand upon their heads!
I hope I'm ready for the worst,
Whatever prank betides!

Perhaps the kingdom of Heaven's changed!
I hope the children there
Won't be new-fashioned when I come,
And laugh at me, and stare!

I hope the father in the skies
Will lift his little girl, —
Old-fashioned, naughty, everything, —
Over the stile of pearl!

· XXI ·

AN awful tempest mashed the air,
The clouds were gaunt and few;
A black, as of a spectre's cloak,
Hid heaven and earth from view.

The creatures chuckled on the roofs
And whistled in the air,
And shook their fists and gnashed their teeth,
And swung their frenzied hair.

The morning lit, the birds arose;
The monster's faded eyes
Turned slowly to his native coast,
And peace was Paradise!

·XXII·

AN everywhere of silver,
With ropes of sand
To keep it from effacing
The track called land.

·XXIII·

A BIRD came down the walk:
He did not know I saw;
He bit an angle-worm in halves
And ate the fellow, raw.

And then he drank a dew
From a convenient grass,
And then hopped sidewise to the wall
To let a beetle pass.

He glanced with rapid eyes
That hurried all abroad, —
They looked like frightened beads, I thought
He stirred his velvet head

Like one in danger; cautious,
I offered him a crumb,
And he unrolled his feathers
And rowed him softer home

Than oars divide the ocean,
Too silver for a seam,
Or butterflies, off banks of noon,
Leap, plashless, as they swim.

· XXIV ·

A NARROW fellow in the grass
Occasionally rides;
You may have met him, — did you not?
His notice sudden is.

The grass divides as with a comb,
A spotted shaft is seen;
And then it closes at your feet
And opens further on.

He likes a boggy acre,
A floor too cool for corn.
Yet when a child, and barefoot,
I more than once, at morn,

Have passed, I thought, a whip-lash
Unbraiding in the sun, —
When, stooping to secure it,
It wrinkled, and was gone.

Several of nature's people
I know, and they know me;
I feel for them a transport
Of cordiality;

But never met this fellow,
Attended or alone,
Without a tighter breathing,
And zero at the bone.

· X X V ·

THE mushroom is the elf of plants,
At evening it is not;
At morning in a truffled hut
It stops upon a spot

As if it tarried always;
And yet its whole career
Is shorter than a snake's delay,
And fleeter than a tare.

'Tis vegetation's juggler,
The germ of alibi;
Doth like a bubble antedate,
And like a bubble hie.

I feel as if the grass were pleased
To have it intermit;
The surreptitious scion
Of summer's circumspect.

Had nature any outcast face,
Could she a son contemn,
Had nature an Iscariot,
That mushroom, — it is him.

· X X V I ·

THERE came a wind like a bugle;
It quivered through the grass,
And a green chill upon the heat
So ominous did pass
We barred the windows and the doors

As from an emerald ghost;
The doom's electric moccasin
That very instant passed.
On a strange mob of panting trees,
And fences fled away,

And rivers where the houses ran
The living looked that day.
The bell within the steeple wild
The flying tidings whirled.
How much can come
And much can go,
And yet abide the world!

·XXVII·

A SPIDER sewed at night
Without a light
Upon an arc of white.
If ruff it was of dame
Or shroud of gnome,
Himself, himself inform.
Of immortality
His strategy
Was physiognomy.

·XXVIII·

I KNOW a place where summer strives
With such a practised frost,
She each year leads her daisies back,
Recording briefly, "Lost."

But when the south wind stirs the pools
And struggles in the lanes,
Her heart misgives her for her vow,
And she pours soft refrains

Into the lap of adamant,
And spices, and the dew,
That stiffens quietly to quartz,
Upon her amber shoe.

· XXIX ·

THE one that could repeat the summer day
Were greater than itself, though he
Minutest of mankind might be.
And who could reproduce the sun,
At period of going down —
The lingering and the stain, I mean —
When Orient has been outgrown,
And Occident becomes unknown,
His name remain.

· XXX ·

THE wind tapped like a tired man,
And like a host, "Come in,"
I boldly answered; entered then
My residence within

A rapid, footless guest,
To offer whom a chair
Were as impossible as hand
A sofa to the air.

No bone had he to bind him,
His speech was like the push
Of numerous humming-birds at once
From a superior bush.

His countenance a billow,
His fingers, if he pass,
Let go a music, as of tunes
Blown tremulous in glass.

He visited, still flitting;
Then, like a timid man,
Again he tapped — 'twas flurriedly —
And I became alone.

·XXXI·

NATURE rarer uses yellow
Than another hue;
Saves she all of that for sunsets, —
Prodigal of blue,

Spending scarlet like a woman,
Yellow she affords
Only scantly and selectly,
Like a lover's words.

·XXXII·

THE leaves, like women, interchange
Sagacious confidence;
Somewhat of nods, and somewhat of
Portentous inference,

The parties in both cases
Enjoining secrecy, —
Inviolable compact
To notoriety.

·XXXIII·

HOW happy is the little stone
That rambles in the road alone,
And doesn't care about careers,
And exigencies never fears;
Whose coat of elemental brown

A passing universe put on;
And independent as the sun,
Associates or glows alone,
Fulfilling absolute decree
In casual simplicity.

·XXXIV·

IT sounded as if the streets were running,
And then the streets stood still.
Eclipse was all we could see at the window,
And awe was all we could feel.

By and by the boldest stole out of his covert,
To see if time was there.
Nature was in her beryl apron,
Mixing fresher air.

·XXXV·

THE rat is the concisest tenant.
He pays no rent, —
Repudiates the obligation,
On schemes intent.

Balking our wit
To sound or circumvent,
Hate cannot harm
A foe so reticent.

Neither decree
Prohibits him,
Lawful as
Equilibrium.

· XXXVI ·

FREQUENTLY the woods are pink,
Frequently are brown;
Frequently the hills undress
Behind my native town.

Oft a head is crested
I was wont to see,
And as oft a cranny
Where it used to be.

And the earth, they tell me,
On its axis turned, —
Wonderful rotation
By but twelve performed!

· XXXVII ·

THE wind begun to rock the grass
With threatening tunes and low, —
He flung a menace at the earth,
A menace at the sky.

The leaves unhooked themselves from trees
And started all abroad;
The dust did scoop itself like hands
And throw away the road.

The wagons quickened on the streets,
The thunder hurried slow;
The lightning showed a yellow beak,
And then a livid claw.

The birds put up the bars to nests,
The cattle fled to barns;
There came one drop of giant rain,
And then, as if the hands

That held the dams had parted hold,
The waters wrecked the sky,
But overlooked my father's house,
Just quartering a tree.

·XXXVIII·

SOUTH winds jostle them,
Bumblebees come,
Hover, hesitate,
Drink, and are gone.

Butterflies pause
On their passage Cashmere;
I, softly plucking,
Present them here!

·XXXIX·

BRING me the sunset in a cup,
Reckon the morning's flagons up,
And say how many dew;
Tell me how far the morning leaps,
Tell me what time the weaver sleeps
Who spun the breadths of blue!

Write me how many notes there be
In the new robin's ecstasy
Among astonished boughs;
How many trips the tortoise makes,
How many cups the bee partakes, —
The debauchee of dews!

Also, who laid the rainbow's piers,
Also, who leads the docile spheres
By withes of supple blue?
Whose fingers string the stalactite,
Who counts the wampum of the night,
To see that none is due?

Who built this little Alban house
And shut the windows down so close
My spirit cannot see?
Who'll let me out some gala day,
With implements to fly away,
Passing pomposity?

·XL·

SHE sweeps with many-colored brooms,
And leaves the shreds behind;
Oh, housewife in the evening west,
Come back, and dust the pond!

You dropped a purple ravelling in,
You dropped an amber thread;
And now you've littered all the East
With duds of emerald!

And still she plies her spotted brooms,
And still the aprons fly,
Till brooms fade softly into stars —
And then I come away.

·XLI·

LIKE mighty footlights burned the red
At bases of the trees, —
The far theatricals of day
Exhibiting to these.

'Twas universe that did applaud
While, chiefest of the crowd,
Enabled by his royal dress,
Myself distinguished God.

· XLII ·

WHERE ships of purple gently toss
On seas of daffodil,
Fantastic sailors mingle,
And then — the wharf is still.

· XLIII ·

BLAZING in gold and quenching in purple,
Leaping like leopards to the sky,
Then at the feet of the old horizon
Laying her spotted face, to die;

Stooping as low as the kitchen window,
Touching the roof and tinting the barn,
Kissing her bonnet to the meadow, —
And the juggler of day is gone!

· XLIV ·

FARTHER in summer than the birds,
Pathetic from the grass,
A minor nation celebrates
Its unobtrusive mass.

No ordinance is seen,
So gradual the grace,
A pensive custom it becomes,
Enlarging loneliness.

Antiquest felt at noon
When August, burning low,
Calls forth this spectral canticle,
Repose to typify.

Remit as yet no grace,
No furrow on the glow,
Yet a druidic difference
Enhances nature now.

· XLV ·

AS imperceptibly as grief
The summer lapsed away, —
Too imperceptible, at last,
To seem like perfidy.

A quietness distilled,
As twilight long begun,
Or Nature, spending with herself
Sequestered afternoon.

The dusk drew earlier in,
The morning foreign shone, —
A courteous, yet harrowing grace,
As guest who would be gone.

And thus, without a wing,
Or service of a keel,
Our summer made her light escape
Into the beautiful.

· XLVI ·

IT can't be summer, — that got through;
It's early yet for spring;
There's that long town of white to cross
Before the blackbirds sing.

It can't be dying, — it's too rouge, —
The dead shall go in white.
So sunset shuts my question down
With clasps of chrysolite.

· XLVII ·

THE gentian weaves her fringes,
The maple's loom is red.
My departing blossoms
Obviate parade.

A brief, but patient illness,
An hour to prepare;
And one, below this morning,
Is where the angels are.

It was a short procession, —
The bobolink was there,
An aged bee addressed us,
And then we knelt in prayer.

We trust that she was willing, —
We ask that we may be.
Summer, sister, seraph,
Let us go with thee!

In the name of the bee
And of the butterfly
And of the breeze, amen!

· XLVIII ·

GOD made a little gentian;
It tried to be a rose
And failed, and all the summer laughed.
But just before the snows
There came a purple creature

That ravished all the hill;
And summer hid her forehead,
And mockery was still.
The frosts were her condition;
The Tyrian would not come
Until the North evoked it.
"Creator! shall I bloom?"

· XLIX ·

BESIDES the autumn poets sing,
A few prosaic days
A little this side of the snow
And that side of the haze.

A few incisive mornings,
A few ascetic eves, —
Gone Mr. Bryant's golden-rod,
And Mr. Thomson's sheaves.

Still is the bustle in the brook,
Sealed are the spicy valves;
Mesmeric fingers softly touch
The eyes of many elves.

Perhaps a squirrel may remain,
My sentiments to share.
Grant me, O Lord, a sunny mind,
Thy windy will to bear!

· L ·

IT sifts from leaden sieves,
It powders all the wood,
It fills with alabaster wool
The wrinkles of the road.

It makes an even face
Of mountain and of plain, —
Unbroken forehead from the east
Unto the east again.

It reaches to the fence,
It wraps it, rail by rail,
Till it is lost in fleeces;
It flings a crystal veil

On stump and stack and stem, —
The summer's empty room,
Acres of seams where harvests were,
Recordless, but for them.

It ruffles wrists of posts,
As ankles of a queen, —
Then stills its artisans like ghosts,
Denying they have been.

·LI·

NO brigadier throughout the year
So civic as the Jay.
A neighbor and a warrior too,
With shrill felicity

Pursuing winds that censure us
A February day,
The brother of the universe
Was never blown away.

The snow and he are intimate;
I've often seen them play
When heaven looked upon us all
With such severity,

I felt apology were due
To an insulted sky,
Whose pompous frown was nutriment
To their temerity.

The pillow of this daring head
Is pungent evergreens;
His larder — terse and militant —
Unknown, refreshing things;

His character a tonic,
His future a dispute;
Unfair an immortality
That leaves this neighbor out.

·LII·

NEW feet within my garden go,
New fingers stir the sod;
A troubadour upon the elm
Betrays the solitude.

New children play upon the green,
New weary sleep below;
And still the pensive spring returns,
And still the punctual snow!

·LIII·

PINK, small, and punctual,
Aromatic, low,
Covert in April,
Candid in May,

Dear to the moss,
Known by the knoll,
Next to the robin
In every human soul.

Bold little beauty,
Bedecked with thee,
Nature forswears
Antiquity.

(With the first Arbutus.)

·LIV·

THE murmur of a bee
A witchcraft yieldeth me.
If any ask me why,
'Twere easier to die
Than tell.

The red upon the hill
Taketh away my will;
If anybody sneer,
Take care, for God is here,
That's all.

The breaking of the day
Addeth to my degree;
If any ask me how,
Artist, who drew me so,
Must tell!

·LV·

PERHAPS you'd like to buy a flower?
But I could never sell.
If you would like to borrow
Until the daffodil

Unties her yellow bonnet
Beneath the village door,
Until the bees, from clover rows
Their hock and sherry draw,

Why, I will lend until just then,
But not an hour more!

· LVI ·

THE pedigree of honey
Does not concern the bee;
A clover, any time, to him
Is aristocracy.

· LVII ·

SOME keep the Sabbath going to church;
I keep it staying at home,
With a bobolink for a chorister,
And an orchard for a dome.

Some keep the Sabbath in surplice;
I just wear my wings,
And instead of tolling the bell for church,
Our little sexton sings.

God preaches, — a noted clergyman, —
And the sermon is never long;
So instead of getting to heaven at last,
I'm going all along!

· LVIII ·

THE bee is not afraid of me,
I know the butterfly;
The pretty people in the woods
Receive me cordially.

The brooks laugh louder when I come,
The breezes madder play.
Wherefore, mine eyes, thy silver mists?
Wherefore, O summer's day?

·LIX·

SOME rainbow coming from the fair!
Some vision of the World Cashmere
I confidently see!
Or else a peacock's purple train,
Feather by feather, on the plain
Fritters itself away!

The dreamy butterflies bestir,
Lethargic pools resume the whir
Of last year's sundered tune.
From some old fortress on the sun
Baronial bees march, one by one,
In murmuring platoon!

The robins stand as thick to-day
As flakes of snow stood yesterday,
On fence and roof and twig.
The orchis binds her feather on
For her old lover, Don the Sun,
Revisiting the bog!

Without commander, countless, still,
The regiment of wood and hill
In bright detachment stand.
Behold! Whose multitudes are these?
The children of whose turbaned seas,
Or what Circassian land?

· LX ·

THE grass so little has to do, —
A sphere of simple green,
With only butterflies to brood,
And bees to entertain,

And stir all day to pretty tunes
The breezes fetch along,
And hold the sunshine in its lap
And bow to everything;

And thread the dews all night, like pearls,
And make itself so fine, —
A duchess were too common
For such a noticing.

And even when it dies, to pass
In odors so divine,
As lowly spices gone to sleep,
Or amulets of pine.

And then to dwell in sovereign barns,
And dream the days away, —
The grass so little has to do,
I wish I were a hay!

· LXI ·

A LITTLE road not made of man,
Enabled of the eye,
Accessible to thill of bee,
Or cart of butterfly.

If town it have, beyond itself,
'Tis that I cannot say;
I only sigh, — no vehicle
Bears me along that way.

·LXII·

A DROP fell on the apple tree,
Another on the roof;
A half a dozen kissed the eaves,
And made the gables laugh.

A few went out to help the brook,
That went to help the sea.
Myself conjectured, Were they pearls,
What necklaces could be!

The dust replaced in hoisted roads,
The birds jocoser sung;
The sunshine threw his hat away,
The orchards spangles hung.

The breezes brought dejected lutes,
And bathed them in the glee;
The East put out a single flag,
And signed the fête away.

·LXIII·

A SOMETHING in a summer's day,
As slow her flambeaux burn away,
Which solemnizes me.

A something in a summer's noon, —
An azure depth, a wordless tune,
Transcending ecstasy.

And still within a summer's night
A something so transporting bright,
I clap my hands to see;

Then veil my too inspecting face,
Lest such a subtle, shimmering grace
Flutter too far for me.

The wizard-fingers never rest,
The purple brook within the breast
Still chafes its narrow bed;

Still rears the East her amber flag,
Guides still the sun along the crag
His caravan of red,

Like flowers that heard the tale of dews,
But never deemed the dripping prize
Awaited their low brows;

Or bees, that thought the summer's name
Some rumor of delirium
No summer could for them;

Or Arctic creature, dimly stirred
By tropic hint, — some travelled bird
Imported to the wood;

Or wind's bright signal to the ear,
Making that homely and severe,
Contented, known, before

The heaven unexpected came,
To lives that thought their worshipping
A too presumptuous psalm.

· LXIV ·

THIS is the land the sunset washes,
These are the banks of the Yellow Sea;
Where it rose, or whither it rushes,
These are the western mystery!

Night after night her purple traffic
Strews the landing with opal bales;
Merchantmen poise upon horizons,
Dip, and vanish with fairy sails.

·LXV·

LIKE trains of cars on tracks of plush
I hear the level bee:
A jar across the flowers goes,
Their velvet masonry

Withstands until the sweet assault
Their chivalry consumes,
While he, victorious, tilts away
To vanquish other blooms.

His feet are shod with gauze,
His helmet is of gold;
His breast, a single onyx
With chrysoprase, inlaid.

His labor is a chant,
His idleness a tune;
Oh, for a bee's experience
Of clovers and of noon!

·LXVI·

THERE is a flower that bees prefer,
And butterflies desire;
To gain the purple democrat
The humming-birds aspire.

And whatsoever insect pass,
A honey bears away
Proportioned to his several dearth
And her capacity.

Her face is rounder than the moon,
And ruddier than the gown
Of orchis in the pasture,
Or rhododendron worn.

She doth not wait for June;
Before the world is green
Her sturdy little countenance
Against the wind is seen,

Contending with the grass,
Near kinsman to herself,
For privilege of sod and sun,
Sweet litigants for life.

And when the hills are full,
And newer fashions blow,
Doth not retract a single spice
For pang of jealousy.

Her public is the noon,
Her providence the sun,
Her progress by the bee proclaimed
In sovereign, swerveless tune.

The bravest of the host,
Surrendering the last,
Nor even of defeat aware
When cancelled by the frost.

·LXVII·

PRESENTIMENT is that long shadow on the lawn
Indicative that suns go down;
The notice to the startled grass
That darkness is about to pass.

·LXVIII·

AS children bid the guest good-night,
And then reluctant turn,
My flowers raise their pretty lips,
Then put their nightgowns on.

As children caper when they wake,
Merry that it is morn,
My flowers from a hundred cribs
Will peep, and prance again.

·LXIX·

ANGELS in the early morning
May be seen the dews among,
Stooping, plucking, smiling, flying:
Do the buds to them belong?

Angels when the sun is hottest
May be seen the sands among,
Stooping, plucking, sighing, flying;
Parched the flowers they bear along.

·LXX·

SO bashful when I spied her,
So pretty, so ashamed!
So hidden in her leaflets,
Lest anybody find;

So breathless till I passed her,
So helpless when I turned
And bore her, struggling, blushing,
Her simple haunts beyond!

For whom I robbed the dingle,
For whom betrayed the dell,
Many will doubtless ask me,
But I shall never tell!

·LXXI·

IT makes no difference abroad,
The seasons fit the same,
The mornings blossom into noons,
And split their pods of flame.

Wild-flowers kindle in the woods,
The brooks brag all the day;
No blackbird bates his jargoning
For passing Calvary.

Auto-da-fé and judgment
Are nothing to the bee;
His separation from his rose
To him seems misery.

·LXXII·

THE mountain sat upon the plain
In his eternal chair,
His observation omnifold,
His inquest everywhere.

The seasons prayed around his knees,
Like children round a sire:
Grandfather of the days is he,
Of dawn the ancestor.

·LXXIII·

I'LL tell you how the sun rose, —
A ribbon at a time.
The steeples swam in amethyst,
The news like squirrels ran.

The hills untied their bonnets,
The bobolinks begun.
Then I said softly to myself,
"That must have been the sun!"

. . . . .

But how he set, I know not.
There seemed a purple stile
Which little yellow boys and girls
Were climbing all the while

Till when they reached the other side,
A dominie in gray
Put gently up the evening bars,
And led the flock away.

·LXXIV·

THE butterfly's assumption-gown,
In chrysoprase apartments hung,
    This afternoon put on.

How condescending to descend,
And be of buttercups the friend
    In a New England town!

·LXXV·

OF all the sounds despatched abroad,
There's not a charge to me
Like that old measure in the boughs,
That phraseless melody

The wind does, working like a hand
Whose fingers comb the sky,
Then quiver down, with tufts of tune
Permitted gods and me.

Inheritance it is to us
Beyond the art to earn,
Beyond the trait to take away
By robber, since the gain

Is gotten not of fingers,
And inner than the bone,
Hid golden for the whole of days,
And even in the urn

I cannot vouch the merry dust
Do not arise and play
In some odd pattern of its own
Some quainter holiday.

When winds go round and round in bands,
And thrum upon the door,
And birds take places overhead,
To bear them orchestra,

I crave him grace of summer boughs,
If such an outcast be,
Who never heard that fleshless chant
Rise solemn on the tree,

As if some caravan of sound
Off deserts, in the sky,
Had parted rank,
Then knit, and swept
In seamless company.[1]

[1] This poem, published on page 122 of the Complete Poems, appears now with the three missing stanzas restored as in the original manuscript sent to Susan Gilbert Dickinson, and also as written to Colonel Higginson.

·LXXVI·

APPARENTLY with no surprise
To any happy flower,
The frost beheads it at its play
In accidental power.

The blond assassin passes on,
The sun proceeds unmoved
To measure off another day
For an approving God.

·LXXVII·

'TWAS later when the summer went
Than when the cricket came,
And yet we knew that gentle clock
Meant nought but going home.

'Twas sooner when the cricket went
Than when the winter came,
Yet that pathetic pendulum
Keeps esoteric time.

·LXXVIII·

THESE are the days when birds come back,
A very few, a bird or two,
To take a backward look.

These are the days when skies put on
The old, old sophistries of June, —
A blue and gold mistake.

Oh, fraud that cannot cheat the bee,
Almost thy plausibility
Induces my belief,

Till ranks of seeds their witness bear,
And softly through the altered air
Hurries a timid leaf!

Oh, sacrament of summer days,
Oh, last communion in the haze,
Permit a child to join,

Thy sacred emblems to partake,
Thy consecrated bread to break,
Taste thine immortal wine!

·LXXIX·

THE morns are meeker than they were,
The nuts are getting brown;
The berry's cheek is plumper,
The rose is out of town.

The maple wears a gayer scarf,
The field a scarlet gown.
Lest I should be old-fashioned,
I'll put a trinket on.

·LXXX·

THE sky is low, the clouds are mean,
A travelling flake of snow
Across a barn or through a rut
Debates if it will go.

A narrow wind complains all day
How some one treated him;
Nature, like us, is sometimes caught
Without her diadem.

·LXXXI·

I THINK the hemlock likes to stand
Upon a marge of snow;
It suits his own austerity,
And satisfies an awe

That men must slake in wilderness,
Or in the desert cloy, —
An instinct for the hoar, the bald,
Lapland's necessity.

The hemlock's nature thrives on cold;
The gnash of northern winds
Is sweetest nutriment to him,
His best Norwegian wines.

To satin races he is nought;
But children on the Don
Beneath his tabernacles play,
And Dnieper wrestlers run.

·LXXXII·

THERE'S a certain slant of light,
On winter afternoons,
That oppresses, like the weight
Of cathedral tunes.

Heavenly hurt it gives us;
We can find no scar,
But internal difference
Where the meanings are.

None may teach it anything,
'Tis the seal, despair, —
An imperial affliction
Sent us of the air.

When it comes, the landscape listens,
Shadows hold their breath;
When it goes, 'tis like the distance
On the look of death.

·LXXXIII·

IT will be Summer eventually —
Ladies with parasols,
Sauntering gentlemen with canes,
And little girls with dolls

Will tint the pallid landscape
As 'twere a bright bouquet,
Though drifted deep in Parian
The village lies to-day.

The lilacs, bending many a year,
Will sway with purple load;
The bees will not despise the tune
Their forefathers have hummed;

The wild rose redden in the bog,
The aster on the hill
Her everlasting fashion set,
And covenant gentians frill,

Till summer folds her miracle
As women do their gown,
Or priests adjust the symbols
When sacrament is done.

LXXXIV.

SHE slept beneath a tree
Remembered but by me.
I touched her cradle mute;
She recognized the foot,
Put on her carmine suit, —
And see!

(With a Tulip.)

LXXXV.

A LIGHT exists in spring
Not present on the year
At any other period.
When March is scarcely here

A color stands abroad
On solitary hills
That science cannot overtake,
But human nature *feels*.

It waits upon the lawn;
It shows the furthest tree
Upon the furthest slope we know;
It almost speaks to me.

Then, as horizons step,
Or noons report away,
Without the formula of sound,
It passes, and we stay:

A quality of loss
Affecting our content,
As trade had suddenly encroached
Upon a sacrament.

· LXXXVI ·

A LADY red upon the hill
Her annual secret keeps;
A lady white within the field
In placid lily sleeps!

The tidy breezes with their brooms
Sweep vale, and hill, and tree!
Prithee, my pretty housewives!
Who may expected be?

The neighbors do not yet suspect!
The woods exchange a smile —
Orchard, and buttercup, and bird —
In such a little while!

And yet how still the landscape stands,
How nonchalant the wood,
As if the resurrection
Were nothing very odd!

· LXXXVII ·

DEAR March, come in!
How glad I am!
I looked for you before.
Put down your hat —
You must have walked —
How out of breath you are!
Dear March, how are you?
And the rest?
Did you leave Nature well?
Oh, March, come right upstairs with me,
I have so much to tell!

I got your letter, and the bird's;
The maples never knew
That you were coming, — I declare,
How red their faces grew!
But, March, forgive me —
And all those hills
You left for me to hue;
There was no purple suitable,
You took it all with you.

Who knocks? That April!
Lock the door!
I will not be pursued!
He stayed away a year, to call
When I am occupied.
But trifles look so trivial
As soon as you have come,
That blame is just as dear as praise
And praise as mere as blame.

·LXXXVIII·

WE like March, his shoes are purple,
He is new and high;
Makes he mud for dog and peddler,
Makes he forest dry;
Knows the adder's tongue his coming,
And begets her spot.
Stands the sun so close and mighty
That our minds are hot.
News is he of all the others;
Bold it were to die
With the blue-birds buccaneering
On his British sky.

·LXXXIX·

NOT knowing when the dawn will come
I open every door;
Or has it feathers like a bird,
Or billows like a shore?

·XC·

A MURMUR in the trees to note,
Not loud enough for wind;
A star not far enough to seek,
Nor near enough to find;

A long, long yellow on the lawn,
A hubbub as of feet;
Not audible, as ours to us,
But dapperer, more sweet;

A hurrying home of little men
To houses unperceived, —
All this, and more, if I should tell,
Would never be believed.

Of robins in the trundle bed
How many I espy
Whose nightgowns could not hide the wings,
Although I heard them try!

But then I promised ne'er to tell;
How could I break my word?
So go your way and I'll go mine, —
No fear you'll miss the road.

· XCI ·

MORNING is the place for dew,
Corn is made at noon,
After dinner light for flowers,
Dukes for setting sun!

· XCII ·

TO my quick ear the leaves conferred;
The bushes they were bells;
I could not find a privacy
From Nature's sentinels.

In cave if I presumed to hide,
The walls began to tell;
Creation seemed a mighty crack
To make me visible.

· XCIII ·

A SEPAL, petal, and a thorn
Upon a common summer's morn,
A flash of dew, a bee or two,
A breeze
A caper in the trees, —
And I'm a rose!

· XCIV ·

HIGH from the earth I heard a bird;
He trod upon the trees
As he esteemed them trifles,
And then he spied a breeze,
And situated softly
Upon a pile of wind
Which in a perturbation
Nature had left behind.

A joyous-going fellow
  I gathered from his talk,
Which both of benediction
  And badinage partook,
Without apparent burden,
  I learned, in leafy wood
He was the faithful father
  Of a dependent brood;
And this untoward transport
  His remedy for care, —
A contrast to our respites.
  How different we are!

· XCV ·

THE spider as an artist
  Has never been employed
Though his surpassing merit
  Is freely certified

By every broom and Bridget
  Throughout a Christian land.
Neglected son of genius,
  I take thee by the hand.

· XCVI ·

WHAT mystery pervades a well!
  The water lives so far,
Like neighbor from another world
  Residing in a jar.

The grass does not appear afraid;
  I often wonder he
Can stand so close and look so bold
  At what is dread to me.

Related somehow they may be, —
The sedge stands next the sea,
Where he is floorless, yet of fear
No evidence gives he.

But nature is a stranger yet;
The ones that cite her most
Have never passed her haunted house,
Nor simplified her ghost.

To pity those that know her not
Is helped by the regret
That those who know her, know her less
The nearer her they get.

· XCVII ·

TO make a prairie it takes a clover and one bee, —
And revery.
The revery alone will do
If bees are few.

· XCVIII ·

IT'S like the light, —
A fashionless delight,
It's like the bee, —
A dateless melody.

It's like the woods,
Private like breeze,
Phraseless, yet it stirs
The proudest trees.

It's like the morning, —
Best when it's done, —
The everlasting clocks
Chime noon.

· XCIX ·

A DEW sufficed itself
And satisfied a leaf,
And felt, "how vast a destiny!
How trivial is life!"

The sun went out to work,
The day went out to play,
But not again that dew was seen
By physiognomy.

Whether by day abducted,
Or emptied by the sun
Into the sea, in passing,
Eternally unknown.

· C ·

HIS bill an auger is,
His head, a cap and frill.
He laboreth at every tree, —
A worm his utmost goal.

· CI ·

SWEET is the swamp with its secrets,
Until we meet a snake;
'Tis then we sigh for houses,
And our departure take

At that enthralling gallop
 That only childhood knows.
A snake is summer's treason,
 And guile is where it goes.

·CII·

COULD I but ride indefinite,
 As doth the meadow-bee,
And visit only where I liked,
 And no man visit me,

And flirt all day with buttercups,
 And marry whom I may,
And dwell a little everywhere,
 Or better, run away

With no police to follow,
 Or chase me if I do,
Till I should jump peninsulas
 To get away from you, —

I said, but just to be a bee
 Upon a raft of air,
And row in nowhere all day long,
 And anchor off the bar, —
What liberty! So captives deem
 Who tight in dungeons are.

·CIII·

THE moon was but a chin of gold
 A night or two ago,
And now she turns her perfect face
 Upon the world below.

Her forehead is of amplest blond;
  Her cheek like beryl stone;
Her eye unto the summer dew
  The likest I have known.

Her lips of amber never part;
  But what must be the smile
Upon her friend she could bestow
  Were such her silver will!

And what a privilege to be
  But the remotest star!
For certainly her way might pass
  Beside your twinkling door.

Her bonnet is the firmament,
  The universe her shoe,
The stars the trinkets at her belt,
  Her dimities of blue.

· CIV ·

THE bat is dun with wrinkled wings
  Like fallow article,
And not a song pervades his lips,
  Or none perceptible.

His small umbrella, quaintly halved,
  Describing in the air
An arc alike inscrutable, —
  Elate philosopher!

Deputed from what firmament
  Of what astute abode,
Empowered with what malevolence
  Auspiciously withheld.

To his adroit Creator
  Ascribe no less the praise;
Beneficent, believe me,
  His eccentricities.

· CV ·

YOU'VE seen balloons set, haven't you?
  So stately they ascend
It is as swans discarded you
  For duties diamond.

Their liquid feet go softly out
  Upon a sea of blond;
They spurn the air as 'twere too mean
  For creatures so renowned.

Their ribbons just beyond the eye,
  They struggle some for breath,
And yet the crowd applauds below;
  They would not encore death.

The gilded creature strains and spins,
  Trips frantic in a tree,
Tears open her imperial veins
  And tumbles in the sea.

The crowd retire with an oath,
  The dust in streets goes down,
And clerks in counting-rooms observe,
  " 'Twas only a balloon."

· CVI ·

THE cricket sang,
  And set the sun,
And workmen finished, one by one,
  Their seam the day upon.

The low grass loaded with the dew,
The twilight stood as strangers do
With hat in hand, polite and new,
To stay as if, or go.

A vastness, as a neighbor, came, —
A wisdom without face or name,
A peace, as hemispheres at home, —
And so the night became.

· CVII ·

DRAB habitation of whom?
Tabernacle or tomb,
Or dome of worm,
Or porch of gnome,
Or some elf's catacomb?
(Sent with a cocoon to her little nephew.)

· CVIII ·

A SLOOP of amber slips away
Upon an ether sea,
And wrecks in peace a purple tar,
The son of ecstasy.

· CIX ·

OF bronze and blaze
The north, to-night!
So adequate its forms,
So preconcerted with itself,
So distant to alarms, —
An unconcern so sovereign
To universe, or me,

It paints my simple spirit
  With tints of majesty,
Till I take vaster attitudes,
  And strut upon my stem,
Disdaining men and oxygen,
  For arrogance of them.

My splendors are menagerie;
  But their competeless show
Will entertain the centuries
  When I am, long ago,
An island in dishonored grass,
  Whom none but daisies know.

· CX ·

HOW the old mountains drip with sunset,
  And the brake of dun!
How the hemlocks are tipped in tinsel
  By the wizard sun!

How the old steeples hand the scarlet,
  Till the ball is full, —
Have I the lip of the flamingo
  That I dare to tell?

Then, how the fire ebbs like billows,
  Touching all the grass
With a departing, sapphire feature,
  As if a duchess pass!

How a small dusk crawls on the village
  Till the houses blot;
And the odd flambeaux no men carry
  Glimmer on the spot!

Now it is night in nest and kennel,
  And where was the wood,
Just a dome of abyss is nodding
  Into solitude! —

These are the visions baffled Guido;
  Titian never told;
Domenichino dropped the pencil,
  Powerless to unfold.

· CXI ·

THE murmuring of bees has ceased;
  But murmuring of some
Posterior, prophetic,
  Has simultaneous come, —
The lower metres of the year,
  When nature's laugh is done, —
The Revelations of the book
  Whose Genesis is June.

PART THREE

LOVE

IT'S all I have to bring to-day,
This, and my heart beside,
This, and my heart, and all the fields,
And all the meadows wide.
Be sure you count, should I forget,—
Some one the sum could tell,—
This, and my heart, and all the bees
Which in the clover dwell.

· I ·

MINE by the right of the white election!
Mine by the royal seal!
Mine by the sign in the scarlet prison
Bars cannot conceal!

Mine, here in vision and in veto!
Mine, by the grave's repeal
Titled, confirmed, — delirious charter!
Mine, while the ages steal!

· II ·

YOU left me, sweet, two legacies, —
A legacy of love
A Heavenly Father would content,
Had He the offer of;

You left me boundaries of pain
Capacious as the sea,
Between eternity and time,
Your consciousness and me.

· III ·

ALTER? When the hills do.
Falter? When the sun
Question if his glory
Be the perfect one.

Surfeit? When the daffodil
Doth of the dew:
Even as herself, O friend!
I will of you!

· IV ·

ELYSIUM is as far as to
The very nearest room,
If in that room a friend await
Felicity or doom.

What fortitude the soul contains,
That it can so endure
The accent of a coming foot,
The opening of a door!

· V ·

DOUBT me, my dim companion!
Why, God would be content
With but a fraction of the love
Poured thee without a stint.
The whole of me, forever,
What more the woman can, —
Say quick, that I may dower thee
With last delight I own!

It cannot be my spirit,
For that was thine before;
I ceded all of dust I knew, —
What opulence the more
Had I, a humble maiden,
Whose farthest of degree
Was that she might
Some distant heaven,
Dwell timidly with thee!

· VI ·

IF you were coming in the fall,
I'd brush the summer by
With half a smile and half a spurn,
As housewives do a fly.

If I could see you in a year,
I'd wind the months in balls,
And put them each in separate drawers,
Until their time befalls.

If only centuries delayed,
I'd count them on my hand,
Subtracting till my fingers dropped
Into Van Diemen's land.

If certain, when this life was out,
That yours and mine should be,
I'd toss it yonder like a rind,
And taste eternity.

But now, all ignorant of the length
Of time's uncertain wing,
It goads me, like the goblin bee,
That will not state its sting.

·VII·

I HIDE myself within my flower,
That wearing on your breast,
You, unsuspecting, wear me too —
And angels know the rest.

I hide myself within my flower,
That, fading from your vase,
You, unsuspecting, feel for me
Almost a loneliness.

·VIII·

THAT I did always love,
I bring thee proof:
That till I loved
I did not love enough.

That I shall love alway,
I offer thee
That love is life,
And life hath immortality.

This, dost thou doubt, sweet?
Then have I
Nothing to show
But Calvary.

· IX ·

HAVE you got a brook in your little heart,
Where bashful flowers blow,
And blushing birds go down to drink,
And shadows tremble so?

And nobody knows, so still it flows,
That any brook is there;
And yet your little draught of life
Is daily drunken there.

Then look out for the little brook in March,
When the rivers overflow,
And the snows come hurrying from the hills,
And the bridges often go.

And later, in August it may be,
When the meadows parching lie,
Beware, lest this little brook of life
Some burning noon go dry!

· X ·

AS if some little Arctic flower,
Upon the polar hem,
Went wandering down the latitudes,
Until it puzzled came

To continents of summer,
To firmaments of sun,
To strange, bright crowds of flowers,
And birds of foreign tongue!
I say, as if this little flower
To Eden wandered in —
What then? Why, nothing, only
Your inference therefrom!

·XI·

MY river runs to thee:
Blue sea, wilt welcome me?

My river waits reply.
Oh sea, look graciously!

I'll fetch thee brooks
From spotted nooks, —

Say, sea,
Take me!

·XII·

I CANNOT live with you,
It would be life,
And life is over there
Behind the shelf

The sexton keeps the key to,
Putting up
Our life, his porcelain,
Like a cup

Discarded of the housewife,
Quaint or broken;
A newer Sèvres pleases,
Old ones crack.

I could not die with you,
For one must wait
To shut the other's gaze down, —
You could not.

And I, could I stand by
And see you freeze,
Without my right of frost,
Death's privilege?

Nor could I rise with you,
Because your face
Would put out Jesus',
That new grace

Glow plain and foreign .
On my homesick eye,
Except that you, than he
Shone closer by.

They'd judge us — how?
For you served Heaven, you know,
Or sought to;
I could not,

Because you saturated sight,
And I had no more eyes
For sordid excellence
As Paradise.

And were you lost, I would be,
Though my name
Rang loudest
On the heavenly fame.

And were you saved,
And I condemned to be
Where you were not,
That self were hell to me.

So we must keep apart,
You there, I here,
With just the door ajar
That oceans are,
And prayer,
And that pale sustenance,
Despair!

· XIII ·

THERE came a day at summer's full
Entirely for me;
I thought that such were for the saints,
Where revelations be.

The sun, as common, went abroad,
The flowers, accustomed, blew,
As if no sail the solstice passed
That maketh all things new.

The time was scarce profaned by speech;
The symbol of a word
Was needless, as at sacrament
The wardrobe of our Lord.

Each was to each the sealéd church,
Permitted to commune this time,
Lest we too awkward show
At supper of the Lamb.

The hours slid fast, as hours will,
Clutched tight by greedy hands;
So faces on two decks look back,
Bound to opposing lands.

And so, when all the time had failed,
Without external sound,
Each bound the other's crucifix,
We gave no other bond.

Sufficient troth that we shall rise —
Deposed, at length, the grave —
To that new marriage, justified
Through Calvaries of Love!

· XIV ·

I'M ceded, I've stopped being theirs;
The name they dropped upon my face
With water, in the country church,
Is finished using now,
And they can put it with my dolls,
My childhood, and the string of spools
I've finished threading too.

Baptized before without the choice,
But this time consciously, of grace
Unto supremest name,
Called to my full, the crescent dropped,
Existence's whole arc filled up
With one small diadem.

My second rank, too small the first,
Crowned, crowing on my father's breast,
A half unconscious queen;
But this time, adequate, erect,
With will to choose or to reject,
And I choose — just a throne.

· XV ·

'TWAS a long parting, but the time
For interview had come;
Before the judgment-seat of God,
The last and second time

These fleshless lovers met,
A heaven in a gaze,
A heaven of heavens, the privilege
Of one another's eyes.

No lifetime set on them,
Apparelled as the new
Unborn, except they had beheld,
Born everlasting now.

Was bridal e'er like this?
A paradise, the host,
And cherubim and seraphim
The most familiar guest.

· XVI ·

I'M wife; I've finished that,
That other state;
I'm Czar, I'm woman now:
It's safer so.

How odd the girl's life looks
Behind this soft eclipse!
I think that earth seems so
To those in heaven now.

This being comfort, then
That other kind was pain;
But why compare?
I'm wife! stop there!

·XVII·

SHE rose to his requirement, dropped
The playthings of her life
To take the honorable work
Of woman and of wife.

If aught she missed in her new day
Of amplitude, or awe,
Or first prospective, or the gold
In using wore away,

It lay unmentioned, as the sea
Develops pearl and weed,
But only to himself is known
The fathoms they abide.

·XVIII·

COME slowly, Eden!
Lips unused to thee,
Bashful, sip thy jasmines,
As the fainting bee,

Reaching late his flower,
Round her chamber hums,
Counts his nectars — enters,
And is lost in balms!

· XIX ·

OF all the souls that stand create
I have elected one.
When sense from spirit files away,
And subterfuge is done;

When that which is and that which was
Apart, intrinsic, stand,
And this brief tragedy of flesh
Is shifted like a sand;

When figures show their royal front
And mists are carved away, —
Behold the atom I preferred
To all the lists of clay!

· XX ·

I HAVE no life but this,
To lead it here;
Nor any death, but lest
Dispelled from there;

Nor tie to earths to come,
Nor action new,
Except through this extent,
The realm of you.

· XXI ·

YOUR riches taught me poverty.
Myself a millionaire
In little wealths, — as girls could boast, —
Till broad as Buenos Ayre,

You drifted your dominions
A different Peru;
And I esteemed all poverty,
For life's estate with you.

Of mines I little know, myself,
But just the names of gems, —
The colors of the commonest;
And scarce of diadems

So much that, did I meet the queen,
Her glory I should know:
But this must be a different wealth,
To miss it beggars so.

I'm sure 'tis India all day
To those who look on you
Without a stint, without a blame, —
Might I but be the Jew!

I'm sure it is Golconda,
Beyond my power to deem, —
To have a smile for mine each day,
How better than a gem!

At least, it solaces to know
That there exists a gold,
Although I prove it just in time
Its distance to behold!

It's far, far treasure to surmise,
And estimate the pearl
That slipped my simple fingers through
While just a girl at school!

·XXII·

I GAVE myself to him,
And took himself for pay.
The solemn contract of a life
Was ratified this way.

The wealth might disappoint,
Myself a poorer prove
Than this great purchaser suspect,
The daily own of Love

Depreciate the vision;
But, till the merchant buy,
Still fable, in the isles of spice,
The subtle cargoes lie.

At least, 'tis mutual risk, —
Some found it mutual gain;
Sweet debt of Life, — each night to owe,
Insolvent, every noon.

·XXIII·

"GOING to him! Happy letter! Tell him —
Tell him the page I didn't write;
Tell him I only said the syntax,
And left the verb and the pronoun out.
Tell him just how the fingers hurried,
Then how they waded, slow, slow, slow;
And then you wished you had eyes in your pages,
So you could see what moved them so.

"Tell him it wasn't a practised writer,
You guessed, from the way the sentence toiled;
You could hear the bodice tug, behind you,
As if it held but the might of a child;

You almost pitied it, you, it worked so.
Tell him — No, you may quibble there,
For it would split his heart to know it,
And then you and I were silenter.

"Tell him night finished before we finished,
And the old clock kept neighing 'day!'
And you got sleepy and begged to be ended —
What could it hinder so, to say?
Tell him just how she sealed you, cautious,
But if he ask where you are hid
Until to-morrow, — happy letter!
Gesture, coquette, and shake your head!"

· XXIV ·

THE way I read a letter's this:
'Tis first I lock the door,
And push it with my fingers next,
For transport it be sure.

And then I go the furthest off
To counteract a knock;
Then draw my little letter forth
And softly pick its lock.

Then, glancing narrow at the wall,
And narrow at the floor,
For firm conviction of a mouse
Not exorcised before,

Peruse how infinite I am
To — no one that you know!
And sigh for lack of heaven, — but not
The heaven the creeds bestow.

·XXV·

WILD nights! Wild nights!
Were I with thee,
Wild nights should be
Our luxury!

Futile the winds
To a heart in port, —
Done with the compass,
Done with the chart.

Rowing in Eden!
Ah! the sea!
Might I but moor
To-night in thee!

·XXVI·

THE night was wide, and furnished scant
With but a single star,
That often as a cloud it met
Blew out itself for fear.

The wind pursued the little bush,
And drove away the leaves
November left; then clambered up
And fretted in the eaves.

No squirrel went abroad;
A dog's belated feet
Like intermittent plush were heard
Adown the empty street.

To feel if blinds be fast,
And closer to the fire
Her little rocking-chair to draw,
And shiver for the poor,

The housewife's gentle task.
"How pleasanter," said she
Unto the sofa opposite,
"The sleet than May — no thee!"

· XXVII ·

DID the harebell loose her girdle
To the lover bee,
Would the bee the harebell hallow
Much as formerly?

Did the paradise, persuaded,
Yield her moat of pearl,
Would the Eden be an Eden,
Or the earl an earl?

· XXVIII ·

A CHARM invests a face
Imperfectly beheld, —
The lady dare not lift her veil
For fear it be dispelled.

But peers beyond her mesh,
And wishes, and denies, —
Lest interview annul a want
That image satisfies.

· XXIX ·

THE rose did caper on her cheek,
Her bodice rose and fell,
Her pretty speech, like drunken men,
Did stagger pitiful.

Her fingers fumbled at her work, —
Her needle would not go;
What ailed so smart a little maid
It puzzled me to know,

Till opposite I spied a cheek
That bore another rose;
Just opposite, another speech
That like the drunkard goes;

A vest that, like the bodice, danced
To the immortal tune, —
Till those two troubled little clocks
Ticked softly into one.

· XXX ·

IN lands I never saw, they say,
Immortal Alps look down,
Whose bonnets touch the firmament,
Whose sandals touch the town, —

Meek at whose everlasting feet
A myriad daisies play.
Which, sir, are you, and which am I,
Upon an August day?

· XXXI ·

THE moon is distant from the sea,
And yet with amber hands
She leads him, docile as a boy,
Along appointed sands.

He never misses a degree;
Obedient to her eye,
He comes just so far toward the town,
Just so far goes away.

Oh, Signor, thine the amber hand,
And mine the distant sea, —
Obedient to the least command
Thine eyes impose on me.

·XXXII·

HE put the belt around my life, —
I heard the buckle snap,
And turned away, imperial,
My lifetime folding up
Deliberate, as a duke would do
A kingdom's title-deed, —
Henceforth a dedicated sort,
A member of the cloud.

Yet not too far to come at call,
And do the little toils
That make the circuit of the rest,
And deal occasional smiles
To lives that stoop to notice mine
And kindly ask it in, —
Whose invitation, knew you not
For whom I must decline?

·XXXIII·

I HELD a jewel in my fingers
And went to sleep.
The day was warm, and winds were prosy
I said: " 'Twill keep."

I woke and chid my honest fingers, —
The gem was gone;
And now an amethyst remembrance
Is all I own.

· XXXIV ·

WHAT if I say I shall not wait?
What if I burst the fleshly gate
And pass, escaped, to thee?
What if I file this mortal off,
See where it hurt me, — that's enough, —
And wade in liberty?

They cannot take us any more, —
Dungeons may call, and guns implore;
Unmeaning now, to me,
As laughter was an hour ago,
Or laces, or a travelling show,
Or who died yesterday!

· XXXV ·

PROUD of my broken heart since thou didst break it,
Proud of the pain I did not feel till thee,
Proud of my night since thou with moons dost slake it,
Not to partake thy passion, my humility.

· XXXVI ·

MY worthiness is all my doubt,
His merit all my fear,
Contrasting which, my qualities
Do lowlier appear;

Lest I should insufficient prove
For his beloved need,
The chiefest apprehension
Within my loving creed.

So I, the undivine abode
Of his elect content,
Conform my soul as 'twere a church
Unto her sacrament.

·XXXVII·

LOVE is anterior to life,
  Posterior to death,
Initial of creation, and
  The exponent of breath.

·XXXVIII·

ONE blessing had I, than the rest
  So larger to my eyes
That I stopped gauging, satisfied,
  For this enchanted size.

It was the limit of my dream,
  The focus of my prayer, —
A perfect, paralyzing bliss
  Contented as despair.

I knew no more of want or cold,
  Phantasms both become,
For this new value in the soul,
  Supremest earthly sum.

The heaven below the heaven above
  Obscured with ruddier hue.
Life's latitude leant over-full;
  The judgment perished, too.

Why joys so scantily disburse,
  Why Paradise defer,
Why floods are served to us in bowls, —
  I speculate no more.

· XXXIX ·

WHEN roses cease to bloom, dear,
  And violets are done,
When bumble-bees in solemn flight
  Have passed beyond the sun,

The hand that paused to gather
  Upon this summer's day
Will idle lie, in Auburn, —
  Then take my flower, pray!

· XL ·

SUMMER for thee grant I may be
  When summer days are flown!
Thy music still when whippoorwill
  And oriole are done!

For thee to bloom, I'll skip the tomb
  And sow my blossoms o'er!
Pray gather me, Anemone,
  Thy flower forevermore!

· XLI ·

SPLIT the lark and you'll find the music,
  Bulb after bulb, in silver rolled,
Scantily dealt to the summer morning,
  Saved for your ear when lutes be old.

Loose the flood, you shall find it patent,
  Gush after gush, reserved for you;
Scarlet experiment! sceptic Thomas,
  Now, do you doubt that your bird was true?

·XLII·

TO lose thee, sweeter than to gain
All other hearts I knew.
'Tis true the drought is destitute,
But then I had the dew!

The Caspian has its realms of sand,
Its other realm of sea;
Without the sterile perquisite
No Caspian could be.

·XLIII·

POOR little heart!
Did they forget thee?
Then dinna care! Then dinna care!

Proud little heart!
Did they forsake thee?
Be debonair! Be debonair!

Frail little heart!
I would not break thee:
Could'st credit me? Could'st credit me?

Gay little heart!
Like morning glory
Thou'll wilted be; thou'll wilted be!

·XLIV·

THERE is a word
Which bears a sword
Can pierce an armed man.
It hurls its barbed syllables, —
At once is mute again.

But where it fell
The saved will tell
 On patriotic day,
Some epauletted brother
 Gave his breath away.

Wherever runs the breathless sun,
 Wherever roams the day,
There is its noiseless onset,
 There is its victory!
Behold the keenest marksman!
 The most accomplished shot!
Time's sublimest target
 Is a soul "forgot"!

· XLV ·

I'VE got an arrow here;
 Loving the hand that sent it,
I the dart revere.

Fell, they will say, in "skirmish"!
 Vanquished, my soul will know,
By but a simple arrow
 Sped by an archer's bow.

· XLVI ·

HE fumbles at your spirit
 As players at the keys
Before they drop full music on;
 He stuns you by degrees,

Prepares your brittle substance
 For the ethereal blow,
By fainter hammers, further heard,
 Then nearer, then so slow

Your breath has time to straighten,
Your brain to bubble cool, —
Deals one imperial thunderbolt
That scalps your naked soul.

· XLVII ·

HEART, we will forget him!
You and I, to-night!
You may forget the warmth he gave,
I will forget the light.

When you have done, pray tell me,
That I my thoughts may dim;
Haste! lest while you're lagging,
I may remember him!

· XLVIII ·

FATHER, I bring thee not myself, —
That were the little load;
I bring thee the imperial heart
I had not strength to hold.

The heart I cherished in my own
Till mine too heavy grew,
Yet strangest, heavier since it went,
Is it too large for you?

· XLIX ·

WE outgrow love like other things
And put it in the drawer,
Till it an antique fashion shows
Like costumes grandsires wore.

· L ·

NOT with a club the heart is broken,
Nor with a stone;
A whip, so small you could not see it,
I've known

To lash the magic creature
Till it fell,
Yet that whip's name too noble
Then to tell.

Magnanimous of bird
By boy descried,
To sing unto the stone
Of which it died.

· LI ·

MY friend must be a bird,
Because it flies!
Mortal my friend must be,
Because it dies!
Barbs has it, like a bee.
Ah, curious friend,
Thou puzzlest me!

· LII ·

HE touched me, so I live to know
That such a day, permitted so,
I groped upon his breast.
It was a boundless place to me,
And silenced, as the awful sea
Puts minor streams to rest.

And now, I'm different from before,
As if I breathed superior air,
Or brushed a royal gown;
My feet, too, that had wandered so,
My gypsy face transfigured now
To tenderer renown.

·LIII·

LET me not mar that perfect dream
By an auroral stain,
But so adjust my daily night
That it will come again.

·LIV·

I LIVE with him, I see his face;
I go no more away
For visitor, or sundown;
Death's single privacy,

The only one forestalling mine,
And that by right that he
Presents a claim invisible,
No wedlock granted me.

I live with him, I hear his voice,
I stand alive to-day
To witness to the certainty
Of immortality

Taught me by Time, — the lower way,
Conviction every day, —
That life like this is endless,
Be judgment what it may.

· LV ·

I ENVY seas whereon he rides,
  I envy spokes of wheels
Of chariots that him convey,
  I envy speechless hills

That gaze upon his journey;
  How easy all can see
What is forbidden utterly
  As heaven, unto me!

I envy nests of sparrows
  That dot his distant eaves,
The wealthy fly upon his pane,
  The happy, happy leaves

That just abroad his window
  Have summer's leave to be,
The earrings of Pizarro
  Could not obtain for me.

I envy light that wakes him,
  And bells that boldly ring
To tell him it is noon abroad, —
  Myself his noon could bring,

Yet interdict my blossom
  And abrogate my bee,
Lest noon in everlasting night
  Drop Gabriel and me.

· LVI ·

A SOLEMN thing it was, I said,
  A woman white to be,
And wear, if God should count me fit
  Her hallowed mystery.

A timid thing to drop a life
  Into the purple well,
Too plummetless that it come back
  Eternity until.

·LVII·

TITLE divine is mine
The Wife without
The Sign.
Acute degree
Conferred on me —
Empress of Calvary.
Royal all but the
Crown —
Betrothed, without the swoon
God gives us women
When two hold
Garnet to garnet,
Gold to gold —
Born — Bridalled —
Shrouded —
In a day
Tri-Victory —
  "My Husband"
Women say
Stroking the melody,
Is this the way? [1]

[1] First published in 1924, in the "Life and Letters of Emily Dickinson" page 49.

PART FOUR

TIME AND ETERNITY

· I ·

ONE dignity delays for all,
One mitred afternoon.
None can avoid this purple,
None evade this crown.

Coach it insures, and footmen,
Chamber and state and throng;
Bells, also, in the village,
As we ride grand along.

What dignified attendants,
What service when we pause!
How loyally at parting
Their hundred hats they raise!

How pomp surpassing ermine,
When simple you and I
Present our meek escutcheon,
And claim the rank to die!

· II ·

DELAYED till she had ceased to know,
Delayed till in its vest of snow
Her loving bosom lay.
An hour behind the fleeting breath,
Later by just an hour than death, —
Oh, lagging yesterday!

Could she have guessed that it would be;
Could but a crier of the glee
Have climbed the distant hill;
Had not the bliss so slow a pace, —
Who knows but this surrendered face
Were undefeated still?

Oh, if there may departing be
Any forgot by victory
In her imperial round,
Show them this meek apparelled thing,
That could not stop to be a king,
Doubtful if it be crowned!

·III·

DEPARTED to the judgment,
A mighty afternoon;
Great clouds like ushers leaning,
Creation looking on.

The flesh surrendered, cancelled,
The bodiless begun;
Two worlds, like audiences, disperse
And leave the soul alone.

·IV·

SAFE in their alabaster chambers,
Untouched by morning and untouched by noon,
Sleep the meek members of the resurrection,
Rafter of satin, and roof of stone.

Light laughs the breeze in her castle of sunshine;
Babbles the bee in a stolid ear;
Pipe the sweet birds in ignorant cadence, —
Ah, what sagacity perished here!

Grand go the years in the crescent above them;
Worlds scoop their arcs, and firmaments row,
Diadems drop and Doges surrender,
Soundless as dots on a disk of snow.

· V ·

ON this long storm the rainbow rose,
On this late morn the sun;
The clouds, like listless elephants,
Horizons straggled down.

The birds rose smiling in their nests,
The gales indeed were done;
Alas! how heedless were the eyes
On whom the summer shone!

The quiet nonchalance of death
No daybreak can bestir;
The slow archangel's syllables
Must awaken her.

· VI ·

MY cocoon tightens, colors tease,
I'm feeling for the air;
A dim capacity for wings
Degrades the dress I wear.

A power of butterfly must be
The aptitude to fly,
Meadows of majesty concedes
And easy sweeps of sky.

So I must baffle at the hint
And cipher at the sign,
And make much blunder, if at last
I take the clew divine.

· VII ·

EXULTATION is the going
Of an inland soul to sea, —
Past the houses, past the headlands,
Into deep eternity!

Bred as we, among the mountains,
Can the sailor understand
The divine intoxication
Of the first league out from land?

· VIII ·

LOOK back on time with kindly eyes,
He doubtless did his best;
How softly sinks his trembling sun
In human nature's west!

· IX ·

A TRAIN went through a burial gate,
A bird broke forth and sang,
And trilled, and quivered, and shook his throat
Till all the churchyard rang;

And then adjusted his little notes,
And bowed and sang again.
Doubtless, he thought it meet of him
To say good-by to men.

· X ·

I DIED for beauty, but was scarce
Adjusted in the tomb,
When one who died for truth was lain
In an adjoining room.

He questioned softly why I failed?
"For beauty," I replied.
"And I for truth, — the two are one;
We brethren are," he said.

And so, as kinsmen met a night,
We talked between the rooms,
Until the moss had reached our lips,
And covered up our names.

· XI ·

HOW many times these low feet staggered,
Only the soldered mouth can tell;
Try! can you stir the awful rivet?
Try! can you lift the hasps of steel?

Stroke the cool forehead, hot so often,
Lift, if you can, the listless hair;
Handle the adamantine fingers
Never a thimble more shall wear.

Buzz the dull flies on the chamber window;
Brave shines the sun through the freckled pane;
Fearless the cobweb swings from the ceiling —
Indolent housewife, in daisies lain!

· XII ·

I LIKE a look of agony,
Because I know it's true;
Men do not sham convulsion,
Nor simulate a throe.

The eyes glaze once, and that is death.
Impossible to feign
The beads upon the forehead
By homely anguish strung.

· XIII ·

THAT short, potential stir
That each can make but once,
That bustle so illustrious
'Tis almost consequence,

Is the *éclat* of death.
Oh, thou unknown renown
That not a beggar would accept,
Had he the power to spurn!

· XIV ·

I WENT to thank her,
But she slept;
Her bed a funnelled stone,
With nosegays at the head and foot,
That travellers had thrown,

Who went to thank her;
But she slept.
'Twas short to cross the sea
To look upon her like, alive,
But turning back 'twas slow.

· XV ·

I'VE seen a dying eye
Run round and round a room
In search of something, as it seemed,
Then cloudier become;

And then, obscure with fog,
And then be soldered down,
Without disclosing what it be,
'Twere blessed to have seen.

· XVI ·

THE clouds their backs together laid,
The north begun to push,
The forests galloped till they fell,
The lightning skipped like mice;
The thunder crumbled like a stuff —
How good to be safe in tombs,
Where nature's temper cannot reach,
Nor vengeance ever comes!

· XVII ·

I NEVER saw a moor,
I never saw the sea;
Yet know I how the heather looks,
And what a wave must be.

I never spoke with God,
Nor visited in heaven;
Yet certain am I of the spot
As if the chart were given.

· XVIII ·

GOD permits industrious angels
Afternoons to play.
I met one, — forgot my school-mates,
All, for him, straightway.

God calls home the angels promptly
At the setting sun;
I missed mine. How dreary marbles,
After playing Crown!

· XIX ·

TO know just how he suffered would be dear;
To know if any human eyes were near
To whom he could intrust his wavering gaze,
Until it settled firm on Paradise.

To know if he was patient, part content,
Was dying as he thought, or different;
Was it a pleasant day to die,
And did the sunshine face his way?

What was his furthest mind, of home, or God,
Or what the distant say
At news that he ceased human nature
On such a day?

And wishes, had he any?
Just his sigh, accented,
Had been legible to me.
And was he confident until
Ill fluttered out in everlasting well?

And if he spoke, what name was best,
What first,
What one broke off with
At the drowsiest?

Was he afraid, or tranquil?
Might he know
How conscious consciousness could grow,
Till love that was, and love too blest to be,
Meet — and the junction be Eternity?

· XX ·

THE last night that she lived,
It was a common night,
Except the dying; this to us
Made nature different.

We noticed smallest things, —
Things overlooked before,
By this great light upon our minds
Italicized, as 'twere.

That others could exist
While she must finish quite,
A jealousy for her arose
So nearly infinite.

We waited while she passed;
It was a narrow time,
Too jostled were our souls to speak,
At length the notice came.

She mentioned, and forgot;
Then lightly as a reed
Bent to the water, shivered scarce,
Consented, and was dead.

And we, we placed the hair,
And drew the head erect;
And then an awful leisure was,
Our faith to regulate.

·XXI·

NOT in this world to see his face
Sounds long, until I read the place
Where this is said to be
But just the primer to a life
Unopened, rare, upon the shelf,
Clasped yet to him and me.

And yet, my primer suits me so
I would not choose a book to know
Than that, be sweeter wise;
Might some one else so learned be,
And leave me just my A B C,
Himself could have the skies.

·XXII·

THE bustle in a house
The morning after death
Is solemnest of industries
Enacted upon earth, —

The sweeping up the heart,
And putting love away
We shall not want to use again
Until eternity.

·XXIII·

I REASON, earth is short,
And anguish absolute,
And many hurt;
But what of that?

I reason, we could die:
The best vitality
Cannot excel decay;
But what of that?

I reason that in heaven
Somehow, it will be even,
Some new equation given;
But what of that?

·XXIV·

AFRAID? Of whom am I afraid?
Not death; for who is he?
The porter of my father's lodge
As much abasheth me.

Of life? 'Twere odd I fear a thing
That comprehendeth me
In one or more existences
At Deity's decree.

Of resurrection? Is the east
Afraid to trust the morn
With her fastidious forehead?
As soon impeach my crown!

·XXV·

THE sun kept setting, setting still;
No hue of afternoon
Upon the village I perceived, —
From house to house 'twas noon.

The dusk kept dropping, dropping still;
No dew upon the grass,
But only on my forehead stopped,
And wandered in my face.

My feet kept drowsing, drowsing still,
My fingers were awake;
Yet why so little sound myself
Unto my seeming make?

How well I knew the light before!
I could not see it now.
'Tis dying, I am doing; but
I'm not afraid to know.

· XXVI ·

TWO swimmers wrestled on the spar
Until the morning sun,
When one turned smiling to the land.
O God, the other one!

The stray ships passing spied a face
Upon the waters borne,
With eyes in death still begging raised,
And hands beseeching thrown.

· XXVII ·

BECAUSE I could not stop for Death,
He kindly stopped for me;
The carriage held but just ourselves
And Immortality.

We slowly drove, he knew no haste,
And I had put away
My labor, and my leisure too,
For his civility.

We passed the school where children played
At wrestling in a ring;
We passed the fields of gazing grain,
We passed the setting sun.

We paused before a house that seemed
A swelling of the ground;
The roof was scarcely visible,
The cornice but a mound.

Since then 'tis centuries; but each
Feels shorter than the day
I first surmised the horses' heads
Were toward eternity.

·XXVIII·

SHE went as quiet as the dew
From a familiar flower.
Not like the dew did she return
At the accustomed hour!

She dropt as softly as a star
From out my summer's eve;
Less skillful than Leverrier
It's sorer to believe!

· XXIX ·

AT last to be identified!
At last, the lamps upon thy side,
The rest of life to see!
Past midnight, past the morning star!
Past sunrise! Ah! what leagues there are
Between our feet and day!

· XXX ·

EXCEPT to heaven, she is nought;
Except for angels, lone;
Except to some wide-wandering bee,
A flower superfluous blown;

Except for winds, provincial;
Except by butterflies,
Unnoticed as a single dew
That on the acre lies.

The smallest housewife in the grass,
Yet take her from the lawn,
And somebody has lost the face
That made existence home!

· XXXI ·

DEATH is a dialogue between
The spirit and the dust.
"Dissolve," says Death. The Spirit, "Sir,
I have another trust."

Death doubts it, argues from the ground.
The Spirit turns away,
Just laying off, for evidence,
An overcoat of clay.

· X X X I I ·

IT was too late for man,
But early yet for God;
Creation impotent to help,
But prayer remained our side.

How excellent the heaven,
When earth cannot be had;
How hospitable, then, the face
Of our old neighbor, God!

· X X X I I I ·

WHEN I was small, a woman died.
To-day her only boy
Went up from the Potomac,
His face all victory,

To look at her; how slowly
The seasons must have turned
Till bullets clipt an angle,
And he passed quickly round!

If pride shall be in Paradise
I never can decide;
Of their imperial conduct,
No person testified.

But proud in apparition,
That woman and her boy
Pass back and forth before my brain,
As ever in the sky.

· XXXIV ·

THE daisy follows soft the sun,
And when his golden walk is done,
Sits shyly at his feet.
He, waking, finds the flower near.
"Wherefore, marauder, art thou here?"
"Because, sir, love is sweet!"

We are the flower, Thou the sun!
Forgive us, if as days decline,
We nearer steal to Thee, —
Enamoured of the parting west,
The peace, the flight, the amethyst,
Night's possibility!

· XXXV ·

NO rack can torture me,
My soul's at liberty.
Behind this mortal bone
There knits a bolder one

You cannot prick with saw,
Nor rend with scimitar.
Two bodies therefore be;
Bind one, and one will flee.

The eagle of his nest
No easier divest
And gain the sky,
Than mayest thou,

Except thyself may be
Thine enemy;
Captivity is consciousness,
So's liberty.

·XXXVI·

I LOST a world the other day.
Has anybody found?
You'll know it by the row of stars
Around its forehead bound.

A rich man might not notice it;
Yet to my frugal eye
Of more esteem than ducats.
Oh, find it, sir, for me!

·XXXVII·

IF I shouldn't be alive
When the robins come,
Give the one in red cravat
A memorial crumb.

If I couldn't thank you,
Being just asleep,
You will know I'm trying
With my granite lip!

·XXXVIII·

SLEEP is supposed to be,
By souls of sanity,
The shutting of the eye.

Sleep is the station grand
Down which on either hand
The hosts of witness stand!

Morn is supposed to be,
By people of degree,
The breaking of the day.

Morning has not occurred!
That shall aurora be
East of eternity;

One with the banner gay,
One in the red array, —
That is the break of day.

· XXXIX ·

I SHALL know why, when time is over,
And I have ceased to wonder why;
Christ will explain each separate anguish
In the fair schoolroom of the sky.

He will tell me what Peter promised,
And I, for wonder at his woe,
I shall forget the drop of anguish
That scalds me now, that scalds me now.

· XL ·

I NEVER lost as much but twice,
And that was in the sod;
Twice have I stood a beggar
Before the door of God!

Angels, twice descending,
Reimbursed my store.
Burglar, banker, father,
I am poor once more!

· XLI ·

LET down the bars, O Death!
The tired flocks come in
Whose bleating ceases to repeat,
Whose wandering is done.

Thine is the stillest night,
Thine the securest fold;
Too near thou art for seeking thee,
Too tender to be told.

·XLII·

GOING to heaven!
I don't know when,
Pray do not ask me how, —
Indeed, I'm too astonished
To think of answering you!
Going to heaven! —
How dim it sounds!
And yet it will be done
As sure as flocks go home at night
Unto the shepherd's arm!

Perhaps you're going too!
Who knows?
If you should get there first,
Save just a little place for me
Close to the two I lost!
The smallest "robe" will fit me,
And just a bit of "crown";
For you know we do not mind our dress
When we are going home.

I'm glad I don't believe it,
For it would stop my breath,
And I'd like to look a little more
At such a curious earth!
I am glad they did believe it
Whom I have never found
Since the mighty autumn afternoon
I left them in the ground.

·XLIII·

AT least to pray is left, is left.
O Jesus! in the air
I know not which thy chamber is, —
I'm knocking everywhere.

Thou stirrest earthquake in the South,
And maelstrom in the sea;
Say, Jesus Christ of Nazareth,
Hast thou no arm for me?

·XLIV·

STEP lightly on this narrow spot!
The broadest land that grows
Be not so ample as the breast
These emerald seams enclose.

Step lofty; for this name is told
As far as cannon dwell,
Or flag subsist, or fame export
Her deathless syllable.

·XLV·

MORNS like these we parted;
Noons like these she rose,
Fluttering first, then firmer,
To her fair repose.

Never did she lisp it,
And 'twas not for me;
She was mute from transport,
I, from agony!

Till the evening, nearing,
One the shutters drew —
Quick! a sharper rustling!
And this linnet flew!

· XLVI ·

A DEATH–BLOW is a life-blow to some
Who, till they died, did not alive become;
Who, had they lived, had died, but when
They died, vitality begun.

· XLVII ·

I READ my sentence steadily,
Reviewed it with my eyes,
To see that I made no mistake
In its extremest clause, —

The date, and manner of the shame;
And then the pious form
That "God have mercy" on the soul
The jury voted him.

I made my soul familiar
With her extremity,
That at the last it should not be
A novel agony,

But she and Death, acquainted,
Meet tranquilly as friends,
Salute and pass without a hint —
And there the matter ends.

· XLVIII ·

I HAVE not told my garden yet,
Lest that should conquer me;
I have not quite the strength now
To break it to the bee.

I will not name it in the street,
For shops would stare, that I,
So shy, so very ignorant,
Should have the face to die.

The hillsides must not know it,
Where I have rambled so,
Nor tell the loving forests
The day that I shall go,

Nor lisp it at the table,
Nor heedless by the way
Hint that within the riddle
One will walk to-day!

· XLIX ·

THEY dropped like flakes, they dropped like stars,
Like petals from a rose,
When suddenly across the June
A wind with fingers goes.

They perished in the seamless grass, —
No eye could find the place;
But God on his repealless list
Can summon every face.

· L ·

THE only ghost I ever saw
Was dressed in mechlin, — so;
He wore no sandal on his foot,
And stepped like flakes of snow.
His gait was soundless, like the bird,
But rapid, like the roe;
His fashions quaint, mosaic,
Or, haply, mistletoe.

His conversation seldom,
His laughter like the breeze
That dies away in dimples
Among the pensive trees.
Our interview was transient, —
Of me, himself was shy;
And God forbid I look behind
Since that appalling day!

· LI ·

SOME, too fragile for winter winds,
The thoughtful grave encloses, —
Tenderly tucking them in from frost
Before their feet are cold.

Never the treasures in her nest
The cautious grave exposes,
Building where schoolboy dare not look
And sportsman is not bold.

This covert have all the children
Early aged, and often cold, —
Sparrows unnoticed by the Father;
Lambs for whom time had not a fold.

·LII·

As by the dead we love to sit,
Become so wondrous dear,
As for the lost we grapple,
Though all the rest are here, —

In broken mathematics
We estimate our prize,
Vast, in its fading ratio,
To our penurious eyes!

·LIII·

DEATH sets a thing significant
The eye had hurried by,
Except a perished creature
Entreat us tenderly

To ponder little workmanships
In crayon or in wool,
With "This was last her fingers did,"
Industrious until

The thimble weighed too heavy,
The stitches stopped themselves,
And then 'twas put among the dust
Upon the closet shelves.

A book I have, a friend gave,
Whose pencil, here and there,
Had notched the place that pleased him, —
At rest his fingers are.

Now, when I read, I read not,
For interrupting tears
Obliterate the etchings
Too costly for repairs.

· LIV ·

I WENT to heaven, —
'Twas a small town,
Lit with a ruby,
Lathed with down.
Stiller than the fields
At the full dew,
Beautiful as pictures
No man drew.
People like the moth,
Of mechlin frames,
Duties of gossamer,
And eider names.
Almost contented
I could be
'Mong such unique
Society.

· LV ·

THEIR height in heaven comforts not,
Their glory nought to me;
'Twas best imperfect, as it was;
I'm finite, I can't see.

The house of supposition,
The glimmering frontier
That skirts the acres of perhaps,
To me shows insecure.

The wealth I had contented me;
If 'twas a meaner size,
Then I had counted it until
It pleased my narrow eyes

Better than larger values,
However true their show;
This timid life of evidence
Keeps pleading, "I don't know."

· LVI ·

THERE is a shame of nobleness
Confronting sudden pelf, —
A finer shame of ecstasy
Convicted of itself.

A best disgrace a brave man feels,
Acknowledged of the brave, —
One more "Ye Blessed" to be told;
But this involves the grave.

· LVII ·

A TRIUMPH may be of several kinds.
There's triumph in the room
When that old imperator, Death,
By faith is overcome.

There's triumph of the finer mind
When truth, affronted long,
Advances calm to her supreme,
Her God her only throng.

A triumph when temptation's bribe
Is slowly handed back,
One eye upon the heaven renounced
And one upon the rack.

Severer triumph, by himself
Experienced, who can pass
Acquitted from that naked bar,
Jehovah's countenance!

·LVIII·

POMPLESS no life can pass away;
  The lowliest career
To the same pageant wends its way
  As that exalted here.

How cordial is the mystery!
  The hospitable pall
A "this way" beckons spaciously, —
  A miracle for all!

·LIX·

I NOTICED people disappeared,
When but a little child, —
Supposed they visited remote,
Or settled regions wild.

Now know I they both visited
And settled regions wild,
But did because they died, — a fact
Withheld the little child!

·LX·

I HAD no cause to be awake,
My best was gone to sleep,
And morn a new politeness took
And failed to wake them up,

But called the others clear,
And passed their curtains by.
Sweet morning, when I over-sleep,
Knock, recollect, for me!

I looked at sunrise once,
And then I looked at them,
And wishfulness in me arose
For circumstance the same.

'Twas such an ample peace,
It could not hold a sigh, —
'Twas Sabbath with the bells divorced,
'Twas sunset all the day.

So choosing but a gown
And taking but a prayer,
The only raiment I should need,
I struggled, and was there.

·LXI·

IF anybody's friend be dead,
It's sharpest of the theme
The thinking how they walked alive,
At such and such a time.

Their costume, of a Sunday,
Some manner of the hair, —
A prank nobody knew but them,
Lost, in the sepulchre.

How warm they were on such a day:
You almost feel the date,
So short way off it seems; and now,
They're centuries from that.

How pleased they were at what you said;
You try to touch the smile,
And dip your fingers in the frost:
When was it, can you tell,

You asked the company to tea,
Acquaintance, just a few,
And chatted close with this grand thing
That don't remember you?

Past bows and invitations,
Past interview, and vow,
Past what ourselves can estimate, —
That makes the quick of woe!

·LXII·

OUR journey had advanced;
Our feet were almost come
To that odd fork in Being's road,
Eternity by term.

Our pace took sudden awe,
Our feet reluctant led.
Before were cities, but between,
The forest of the dead.

Retreat was out of hope, —
Behind, a sealéd route,
Eternity's white flag before,
And God at every gate.

·LXIII·

AMPLE make this bed.
Make this bed with awe;
In it wait till judgment break
Excellent and fair.

Be its mattress straight,
Be its pillow round;
Let no sunrise' yellow noise
Interrupt this ground.

· LXIV ·

ON such a night, or such a night,
Would anybody care
If such a little figure
Slipped quiet from its chair,

So quiet, oh, how quiet!
That nobody might know
But that the little figure
Rocked softer, to and fro?

On such a dawn, or such a dawn,
Would anybody sigh
That such a little figure
Too sound asleep did lie

For chanticleer to wake it, —
Or stirring house below,
Or giddy bird in orchard,
Or early task to do?

There was a little figure plump
For every little knoll,
Busy needles, and spools of thread,
And trudging feet from school.

Playmates, and holidays, and nuts,
And visions vast and small.
Strange that the feet so precious charged
Should reach so small a goal!

·LXV·

ESSENTIAL oils are wrung:
The attar from the rose
Is not expressed by suns alone,
It is the gift of screws.

The general rose decays;
But this, in lady's drawer,
Makes summer when the lady lies
In ceaseless rosemary.

·LXVI·

I LIVED on dread; to those who know
The stimulus there is
In danger, other impetus
Is numb and vital-less.

As 'twere a spur upon the soul,
A fear will urge it where
To go without the spectre's aid
Were challenging despair.

·LXVII·

IF I should die,
And you should live,
And time should gurgle on,
And morn should beam,
And noon should burn,
As it has usual done;
If birds should build as early,
And bees as bustling go, —
One might depart at option
From enterprise below!

'Tis sweet to know that stocks will stand
When we with daisies lie,
That commerce will continue,
And trades as briskly fly.
It makes the parting tranquil
And keeps the soul serene,
That gentlemen so sprightly
Conduct the pleasing scene!

·LXVIII·

HER final summer was it,
And yet we guessed it not;
If tenderer industriousness
Pervaded her, we thought

A further force of life
Developed from within, —
When Death lit all the shortness up,
And made the hurry plain.

We wondered at our blindness, —
When nothing was to see
But her Carrara guide-post, —
At our stupidity,

When, duller than our dulness,
The busy darling lay,
So busy was she, finishing,
So leisurely were we!

·LXIX·

ONE need not be a chamber to be haunted,
One need not be a house;
The brain has corridors surpassing
Material place.

Far safer, of a midnight meeting
External ghost,
Than an interior confronting
That whiter host.

Far safer through an Abbey gallop,
The stones achase,
Than, moonless, one's own self encounter
In lonesome place.

Ourself, behind ourself concealed,
Should startle most;
Assassin, hid in our apartment,
Be horror's least.

The prudent carries a revolver,
He bolts the door,
O'erlooking a superior spectre
More near.

·LXX·

SHE died, — this was the way she died;
And when her breath was done,
Took up her simple wardrobe
And started for the sun.

Her little figure at the gate
The angels must have spied,
Since I could never find her
Upon the mortal side.

·LXXI·

WAIT till the majesty of Death
Invests so mean a brow!
Almost a powdered footman
Might dare to touch it now!

Wait till in everlasting robes
This democrat is dressed,
Then prate about "preferment"
And "station" and the rest!

Around this quiet courtier
Obsequious angels wait!
Full royal is his retinue,
Full purple is his state!

A lord might dare to lift the hat
To such a modest clay,
Since that my Lord, "the Lord of lords"
Receives unblushingly!

· LXXII ·

WENT up a year this evening!
I recollect it well!
Amid no bells nor bravos
The bystanders will tell!
Cheerful, as to the village,
Tranquil, as to repose,
Chastened, as to the chapel,
This humble tourist rose.
Did not talk of returning,
Alluded to no time
When, were the gales propitious,
We might look for him;
Was grateful for the roses
In life's diverse bouquet,
Talked softly of new species
To pick another day.
Beguiling thus the wonder,
The wondrous nearer drew;

Hands bustled at the moorings —
The crowd respectful grew.
Ascended from our vision
To countenances new!
A difference, a daisy,
Is all the rest I knew!

·LXXIII·

TAKEN from men this morning,
Carried by men to-day,
Met by the gods with banners
Who marshalled her away.

One little maid from playmates,
One little mind from school, —
There must be guests in Eden;
All the rooms are full.

Far as the east from even,
Dim as the border star, —
Courtiers quaint, in kingdoms,
Our departed are.

·LXXIV·

WHAT inn is this
Where for the night
Peculiar traveller comes?
Who is the landlord?
Where the maids?
Behold, what curious rooms!
No ruddy fires on the hearth,
No brimming tankards flow.
Necromancer, landlord,
Who are these below?

·LXXV·

IT was not death, for I stood up,
And all the dead lie down;
It was not night, for all the bells
Put out their tongues, for noon.

It was not frost, for on my flesh
I felt siroccos crawl, —
Nor fire, for just my marble feet
Could keep a chancel cool.

And yet it tasted like them all;
The figures I have seen
Set orderly, for burial,
Reminded me of mine,

As if my life were shaven
And fitted to a frame,
And could not breathe without a key;
And 'twas like midnight, some,

When everything that ticked has stopped,
And space stares, all around,
Or grisly frosts, first autumn morns,
Repeal the beating ground.

But most like chaos, — stopless, cool, —
Without a chance or spar,
Or even a report of land
To justify despair.

·LXXVI·

I SHOULD not dare to leave my friend,
Because — because if he should die
While I was gone, and I — too late —
Should reach the heart that wanted me;

If I should disappoint the eyes
That hunted, hunted so, to see,
And could not bear to shut until
They "noticed" me — they noticed me;

If I should stab the patient faith
So sure I'd come — so sure I'd come,
It listening, listening, went to sleep
Telling my tardy name, —

My heart would wish it broke before,
Since breaking then, since breaking then,
Were useless as next morning's sun,
Where midnight frosts had lain!

·LXXVII·

GREAT streets of silence led away
To neighborhoods of pause;
Here was no notice, no dissent,
No universe, no laws.

By clocks 'twas morning, and for night
The bells at distance called;
But epoch had no basis here,
For period exhaled.

·LXXVIII·

A THROE upon the features,
A hurry in the breath,
An ecstasy of parting
Denominated "Death," —

An anguish at the mention,
Which, when to patience grown,
I've known permission given
To rejoin its own.

·LXXIX·

OF tribulation these are they
Denoted by the white;
The spangled gowns, a lesser rank
Of victors designate.

All these did conquer; but the ones
Who overcame most times
Wear nothing commoner than snow,
No ornament but palms.

Surrender is a sort unknown
On this superior soil;
Defeat, an outgrown anguish,
Remembered as the mile

Our panting ankle barely gained
When night devoured the road;
But we stood whispering in the house,
And all we said was "Saved!"

·LXXX·

I THINK just how my shape will rise
When I shall be forgiven,
Till hair and eyes and timid head
Are out of sight, in heaven.

I think just how my lips will weigh
With shapeless, quivering prayer
That you, so late, consider me,
The sparrow of your care.

I mind me that of anguish sent,
Some drifts were moved away
Before my simple bosom broke,—
And why not this, if they?

And so, until delirious borne
I con that thing, — "forgiven," —
Till with long fright and longer trust
I drop my heart, unshriven!

· LXXXI ·

AFTER a hundred years
Nobody knows the place, —
Agony, that enacted there,
Motionless as peace.

Weeds triumphant ranged,
Strangers strolled and spelled
At the lone orthography
Of the elder dead.

Winds of summer fields
Recollect the way, —
Instinct picking up the key
Dropped by memory.

· LXXXII ·

LAY this laurel on the one
Too intrinsic for renown.
Laurel! veil your deathless tree, —
Him you chasten, that is he!

· LXXXIII ·

THIS world is not conclusion;
A sequel stands beyond,
Invisible, as music,
But positive, as sound.
It beckons and it baffles;
Philosophies don't know,

And through a riddle, at the last,
  Sagacity must go.
To guess it puzzles scholars;
  To gain it, men have shown
Contempt of generations,
  And crucifixion known.

·LXXXIV·

WE learn in the retreating
  How vast an one
Was recently among us.
  A perished sun

Endears in the departure
  How doubly more
Than all the golden presence
  It was before!

·LXXXV·

THEY say that "time assuages,"—
  Time never did assuage;
An actual suffering strengthens,
  As sinews do, with age.

Time is a test of trouble,
  But not a remedy.
If such it prove, it prove too
  There was no malady.

·LXXXVI·

WE cover thee, sweet face.
  Not that we tire of thee,
But that thyself fatigue of us;
  Remember, as thou flee,
We follow thee until

Thou notice us no more,
And then, reluctant, turn away
To con thee o'er and o'er,
And blame the scanty love
We were content to show,
Augmented, sweet, a hundred fold
If thou would'st take it now.

·LXXXVII·

THAT is solemn we have ended, —
Be it but a play,
Or a glee among the garrets,
Or a holiday,

Or a leaving home; or later,
Parting with a world
We have understood, for better
Still it be unfurled.

·LXXXVIII·

THE stimulus, beyond the grave
His countenance to see,
Supports me like imperial drams
Afforded royalty.

·LXXXIX·

GIVEN in marriage unto thee,
Oh, thou celestial host!
Bride of the Father and the Son,
Bride of the Holy Ghost!

Other betrothal shall dissolve,
Wedlock of will decay;
Only the keeper of this seal
Conquers mortality.

· XC ·

THAT such have died enables us
The tranquiller to die;
That such have lived, certificate
For immortality.

· XCI ·

THEY won't frown always, — some sweet day
When I forget to tease,
They'll recollect how cold I looked,
And how I just said "please."

Then they will hasten to the door
To call the little child,
Who cannot thank them, for the ice
That on her lisping piled.

· XCII ·

'TIS an honorable thought,
And makes one lift one's hat,
As one encountered gentlefolk
Upon a daily street,

That we've immortal place,
Though pyramids decay,
And kingdoms, like the orchard,
Flit russetly away.

· XCIII ·

THE distance that the dead have gone
Does not at first appear;
Their coming back seems possible
For many an ardent year.

And then, that we have followed them
  We more than half suspect,
So intimate have we become
  With their dear retrospect.

· XCIV ·

HOW dare the robins sing,
  When men and women hear
Who since they went to their account
  Have settled with the year! —
Paid all that life had earned
  In one consummate bill,
And now, what life or death can do
  Is immaterial.
Insulting is the sun
  To him whose mortal light,
Beguiled of immortality,
  Bequeaths him to the night.
In deference to him
  Extinct be every hum,
Whose garden wrestles with the dew,
  At daybreak overcome!

· XCV ·

DEATH is like the insect
  Menacing the tree,
Competent to kill it,
  But decoyed may be.

Bait it with the balsam,
  Seek it with the knife,
Baffle, if it cost you
  Everything in life.

Then, if it have burrowed
Out of reach of skill,
Ring the tree and leave it, —
'Tis the vermin's will.

·XCVI·

'TIS sunrise, little maid, hast thou
No station in the day?
'Twas not thy wont to hinder so, —
Retrieve thine industry.

'Tis noon, my little maid, alas!
And art thou sleeping yet?
The lily waiting to be wed,
The bee, dost thou forget?

My little maid, 'tis night; alas,
That night should be to thee
Instead of morning! Hadst thou broached
Thy little plan to me,
Dissuade thee if I could not, sweet,
I might have aided thee.

·XCVII·

EACH that we lose takes part of us;
A crescent still abides,
Which like the moon, some turbid night,
Is summoned by the tides.

·XCVIII·

NOT any higher stands the grave
For heroes than for men;
Not any nearer for the child
Than numb three-score and ten.

This latest leisure equal lulls
The beggar and his queen;
Propitiate this democrat
A summer's afternoon.

·XCIX·

AS far from pity as complaint,
As cool to speech as stone,
As numb to revelation
As if my trade were bone.

As far from time as history,
As near yourself to-day
As children to the rainbow's scarf,
Or sunset's yellow play

To eyelids in the sepulchre.
How still the dancer lies,
While color's revelations break,
And blaze the butterflies!

·C·

'TIS whiter than an Indian pipe,
'Tis dimmer than a lace;
No stature has it, like a fog,
When you approach the place.

Not any voice denotes it here,
Or intimates it there;
A spirit, how doth it accost?
What customs hath the air?

This limitless hyperbole
Each one of us shall be;
'Tis drama, if (hypothesis)
It be not tragedy!

·CI·

SHE laid her docile crescent down,
  And this confiding stone
Still states, to dates that have forgot,
  The news that she is gone.

So constant to its stolid trust,
  The shaft that never knew,
It shames the constancy that fled
  Before its emblem flew.

·CII·

BLESS God, he went as soldiers,
  His musket on his breast;
Grant, God, he charge the bravest
  Of all the martial blest.

Please God, might I behold him
  In epauletted white,
I should not fear the foe then,
  I should not fear the fight.

·CIII·

IMMORTAL is an ample word
  When what we need is by,
But when it leaves us for a time,
  'Tis a necessity.

Of heaven above the firmest proof
  We fundamental know,
Except for its marauding hand,
  It had been heaven below.

· CIV ·

WHERE every bird is bold to go,
And bees abashless play,
The foreigner before he knocks
Must thrust the tears away.

· CV ·

THE grave my little cottage is,
Where, keeping house for thee,
I make my parlor orderly,
And lay the marble tea,

For two divided, briefly,
A cycle, it may be,
Till everlasting life unite
In strong society.

· CVI ·

THIS was in the white of the year,
That was in the green,
Drifts were as difficult then to think
As daisies now to be seen.

Looking back is best that is left,
Or if it be before,
Retrospection is prospect's half,
Sometimes almost more.

· CVII ·

SWEET hours have perished here;
This is a mighty room;
Within its precincts hopes have played, —
Now shadows in the tomb.

·CVIII·

ME! Come! My dazzled face
In such a shining place!

Me! Hear! My foreign ear
The sounds of welcome near!

The saints shall meet
Our bashful feet.

My holiday shall be
That they remember me;

My paradise, the fame
That they pronounce my name.

·CIX·

FROM us she wandered now a year,
  Her tarrying unknown;
If wilderness prevent her feet,
  Or that ethereal zone

No eye hath seen and lived,
  We ignorant must be.
We only know what time of year
  We took the mystery.

·CX·

I WISH I knew that woman's name,
  So, when she comes this way,
To hold my life, and hold my ears,
  For fear I hear her say

She's "sorry I am dead", again,
  Just when the grave and I
Have sobbed ourselves almost to sleep, —
  Our only lullaby.

· CXI ·

BEREAVED of all, I went abroad,
  No less bereaved to be
Upon a new peninsula, —
  The grave preceded me,

Obtained my lodgings ere myself,
  And when I sought my bed,
The grave it was, reposed upon
  The pillow for my head.

I waked, to find it first awake,
  I rose, — it followed me;
I tried to drop it in the crowd,
  To lose it in the sea,

In cups of artificial drowse
  To sleep its shape away, —
The grave was finished, but the spade
  Remained in memory.

· CXII ·

I FELT a funeral in my brain,
  And mourners, to and fro,
Kept treading, treading, till it seemed
  That sense was breaking through.

And when they all were seated,
  A service like a drum
Kept beating, beating, till I thought
  My mind was going numb.

And then I heard them lift a box,
  And creak across my soul
With those same boots of lead, again.
  Then space began to toll

As all the heavens were a bell,
  And Being but an ear,
And I and silence some strange race,
  Wrecked, solitary, here.

·CXIII·

I MEANT to find her when I came;
  Death had the same design;
But the success was his, it seems,
  And the discomfit mine.

I meant to tell her how I longed
  For just this single time;
But Death had told her so the first,
  And she had hearkened him.

To wander now is my abode;
  To rest, — to rest would be
A privilege of hurricane
  To memory and me.

·CXIV·

I SING to use the waiting,
  My bonnet but to tie,
And shut the door unto my house;
  No more to do have I,

Till, his best step approaching,
  We journey to the day,
And tell each other how we sang
  To keep the dark away.

·CXV·

A SICKNESS of this world it most occasions
When best men die;
A wishfulness their far condition
To occupy.

A chief indifference, as foreign
A world must be
Themselves forsake contented,
For Deity.

·CXVI·

SUPERFLUOUS were the sun
When excellence is dead;
He were superfluous every day,
For every day is said

That syllable whose faith
Just saves it from despair,
And whose "I'll meet you" hesitates—
If love inquire, "Where?"

Upon his dateless fame
Our periods may lie,
As stars that drop anonymous
From an abundant sky.

·CXVII·

SO proud she was to die
It made us all ashamed
That what we cherished, so unknown
To her desire seemed.

So satisfied to go
  Where none of us should be,
Immediately, that anguish stooped
  Almost to jealousy.

· CXVIII ·

TIE the strings to my life, my Lord,
  Then I am ready to go!
Just a look at the horses —
  Rapid! That will do!

Put me on the firmest side,
  So I shall never fall;
For we must ride to the Judgment,
  And it's partly down hill.

But never I mind the bridges,
  And never I mind the sea;
Held fast in everlasting race
  By my own choice and thee.

Good-by to the life I used to live,
  And the world I used to know;
And kiss the hills for me, just once;
  Now I am ready to go!

· CXIX ·

THE dying need but little, dear, —
  A glass of water's all,
A flower's unobtrusive face
  To punctuate the wall,

A fan, perhaps, a friend's regret,
  And certainly that one
No color in the rainbow
  Perceives when you are gone.

·CXX·

THERE'S something quieter than sleep
Within this inner room!
It wears a sprig upon its breast,
And will not tell its name.

Some touch it and some kiss it,
Some chafe its idle hand;
It has a simple gravity
I do not understand!

While simple-hearted neighbors
Chat of the "early dead",
We, prone to periphrasis,
Remark that birds have fled!

·CXXI·

THE soul should always stand ajar
That if the heaven inquire,
He will not be obliged to wait,
Or shy of troubling her.

Depart, before the host has slid
The bolt upon the door,
To seek for the accomplished guest —
Her visitor no more.

·CXXII·

THREE weeks passed since I had seen her, —
Some disease had vexed;
'Twas with text and village singing
I beheld her next,

And a company — our pleasure
To discourse alone;
Gracious now to me as any,
Gracious unto none.

Borne, without dissent of either,
To the parish night;
Of the separated people
Which are out of sight?

· CXXIII ·

I BREATHED enough to learn the trick,
And now, removed from air,
I simulate the breath so well,
That one, to be quite sure

The lungs are stirless, must descend
Among the cunning cells,
And touch the pantomime himself.
How cool the bellows feels!

· CXXIV ·

I'M sorry for the Dead to-day,
It's such congenial times
Old neighbors have at fences
At time o' year for hay —

When broad sun-burned acquaintances
Discourse between the toil
And laugh, a homely species,
That makes the meadows smile.

It seems so straight to lie away
From all the noise of fields,
The busy carts, the fragrant cocks;
The mower's metre steals

A trouble, lest they're homesick, —
Those farmers and their wives,
Set separate from the farming
And all the neighbors' lives.

I wonder if the sepulchre
Is not a lonesome way,
When men and boys, and larks and June
Go down the fields to hay! [1]

· CXXV ·

IF tolling bell I ask the cause,
"A soul has gone to God,"
I'm answered in a lonesome tone;
Is heaven then so sad?

That bells should joyful ring to tell
A soul had gone to heaven,
Would seem to me the proper way
A good news should be given.

· CXXVI ·

IF I may have it when it's dead
I will contented be;
If just as soon as breath is out
It shall belong to me,

Until they lock it in the grave,
'Tis bliss I cannot weigh,
For though they lock thee in the grave,
Myself can hold the key.

[1] The last stanza only appeared on page 244 of the "Complete Poems." The entire poem was first published in the appendix of the "Further Poems" in 1929.

Think of it, lover! I and thee
  Permitted face to face to be;
After a life, a death we'll say, —
  For death was that, and this is thee.

· CXXVII ·

BEFORE the ice is in the pools,
  Before the skaters go,
Or any cheek at nightfall
  Is tarnished by the snow,

Before the fields have finished,
  Before the Christmas tree,
Wonder upon wonder
  Will arrive to me!

What we touch the hems of
  On a summer's day;
What is only walking
  Just a bridge away;

That which sings so, speaks so,
  When there's no one here, —
Will the frock I wept in
  Answer me to wear?

· CXXVIII ·

I HEARD a fly buzz when I died;
  The stillness round my form
Was like the stillness in the air
  Between the heaves of storm.

The eyes beside had wrung them dry,
  And breaths were gathering sure
For that last onset, when the king
  Be witnessed in his power.

I willed my keepsakes, signed away
  What portion of me I
Could make assignable, — and then
  There interposed a fly,

With blue, uncertain, stumbling buzz,
  Between the light and me;
And then the windows failed, and then
  I could not see to see.

·CXXIX·

ADRIFT! A little boat adrift!
  And night is coming down!
Will no one guide a little boat
  Unto the nearest town?

So sailors say, on yesterday,
  Just as the dusk was brown,
One little boat gave up its strife,
  And gurgled down and down.

But angels say, on yesterday,
  Just as the dawn was red,
One little boat o'erspent with gales
Retrimmed its masts, redecked its sails
  Exultant, onward sped!

·CXXX·

THERE'S been a death in the opposite house
  As lately as to-day.
I know it by the numb look
  Such houses have alway.

The neighbors rustle in and out,
  The doctor drives away.
A window opens like a pod,
  Abrupt, mechanically;

Somebody flings a mattress out, —
The children hurry by;
They wonder if It died on that, —
I used to when a boy.

The minister goes stiffly in
As if the house were his,
And he owned all the mourners now,
And little boys besides;

And then the milliner, and the man
Of the appalling trade,
To take the measure of the house.
There'll be that dark parade

Of tassels and of coaches soon;
It's easy as a sign, —
The intuition of the news
In just a country town.

· CXXXI ·

WE never know we go, — when we are going
We jest and shut the door;
Fate following behind us bolts it,
And we accost no more.

· CXXXII ·

IT struck me every day
The lightning was as new
As if the cloud that instant slit
And let the fire through.

It burned me in the night,
It blistered in my dream;
It sickened fresh upon my sight
With every morning's beam.

I thought that storm was brief, —
The maddest, quickest by;
But Nature lost the date of this,
And left it in the sky.

·CXXXIII·

WATER is taught by thirst;
Land, by the oceans passed;
Transport, by throe;
Peace, by its battles told;
Love, by memorial mould;
Birds, by the snow.

·CXXXIV·

WE thirst at first, — 'tis Nature's act;
And later, when we die,
A little water supplicate
Of fingers going by.

It intimates the finer want,
Whose adequate supply
Is that great water in the west
Termed immortality.

·CXXXV·

A CLOCK stopped — not the mantel's;
Geneva's farthest skill
Can't put the puppet bowing
That just now dangled still.

An awe came on the trinket!
The figures hunched with pain,
Then quivered out of decimals
Into degreeless noon.

It will not stir for doctors,
This pendulum of snow;
The shopman importunes it,
While cool, concernless No

Nods from the gilded pointers,
Nods from the seconds slim,
Decades of arrogance between
The dial life and him.

·CXXXVI·

ALL overgrown by cunning moss,
All interspersed with weed,
The little cage of "Currer Bell",
In quiet Haworth laid.

This bird, observing others,
When frosts too sharp became,
Retire to other latitudes,
Quietly did the same.

But differed in returning;
Since Yorkshire hills are green,
Yet not in all the nests I meet
Can nightingale be seen.

Gathered from any wanderings,
Gethsemane can tell
Through what transporting anguish
She reached the asphodel!

Soft fall the sounds of Eden
Upon her puzzled ear;
Oh, what an afternoon for heaven,
When Brontë entered there!

·CXXXVII·

A TOAD can die of light!
Death is the common right
Of toads and men, —
Of earl and midge

The privilege.
Why swagger then?
The gnat's supremacy
Is large as thine.

·CXXXVIII·

FAR from love the Heavenly Father
Leads the chosen child;
Oftener through realm of briar
Than the meadow mild,

Oftener by the claw of dragon
Than the hand of friend,
Guides the little one predestined
To the native land.

·CXXXIX·

A LONG, long sleep, a famous sleep
That makes no show for dawn
By stretch of limb or stir of lid, —
An independent one.

Was ever idleness like this?
Within a hut of stone
To bask the centuries away
Nor once look up for noon?

· C X L ·

'TWAS just this time last year I died.
I know I heard the corn,
When I was carried by the farms,—
It had the tassels on.

I thought how yellow it would look
When Richard went to mill;
And then I wanted to get out,
But something held my will.

I thought just how red apples wedged
The stubble's joints between;
And carts went stooping round the fields
To take the pumpkins in.

I wondered which would miss me least,
And when Thanksgiving came,
If father'd multiply the plates
To make an even sum.

And if my stocking hung too high,
Would it blur the Christmas glee,
That not a Santa Claus could reach
The altitude of me?

But this sort grieved myself, and so
I thought how it would be
When just this time, some perfect year,
Themselves should come to me.

· CXLI ·

ON this wondrous sea,
  Sailing silently,
Knowest thou the shore
  Ho! pilot, ho!
Where no breakers roar,
  Where the storm is o'er?

In the silent west
Many sails at rest,
  Their anchors fast;
Thither I pilot thee, —
Land, ho! Eternity!
  Ashore at last!

PART FIVE

THE SINGLE HOUND

ONE Sister have I in our house,
And one a hedge away,
There's only one recorded
But both belong to me.

One came the way that I came
And wore my last year's gown,
The other as a bird her nest,
Builded our hearts among.

She did not sing as we did,
It was a different tune,
Herself to her a music
As Bumble-bee of June.

To-day is far from childhood
But up and down the hills
I held her hand the tighter,
Which shortened all the miles.

And still her hum the years among
Deceives the Butterfly,
Still in her eye the Violets lie
Mouldered this many May.

I spilt the dew but took the morn,
I chose this single star
From out the wide night's numbers,
Sue — forevermore!

EMILY.

· I ·

ADVENTURE most unto itself
The Soul condemned to be;
Attended by a Single Hound —
Its own Identity.

· II ·

THE Soul that has a Guest,
Doth seldom go abroad,
Diviner Crowd at home
Obliterate the need,
And courtesy forbid
A Host's departure, when
Upon Himself be visiting
The Emperor of Men!

· III ·

EXCEPT the smaller size, no Lives are round,
These hurry to a sphere, and show, and end.
The larger, slower grow, and later hang —
The Summers of Hesperides are long.

· IV ·

FAME is a fickle food
Upon a shifting plate,
Whose table once a Guest, but not
The second time, is set.

Whose crumbs the crows inspect,
And with ironic caw
Flap past it to the Farmer's corn;
Men eat of it and die.

·V·

THE right to perish might be thought
An undisputed right,
Attempt it, and the Universe upon the opposite
Will concentrate its officers —
You cannot even die,
But Nature and Mankind must pause
To pay you scrutiny.

·VI·

PERIL as a possession
'Tis good to bear,
Danger disintegrates satiety;
There's Basis there
Begets an awe,
That searches Human Nature's creases
As clean as Fire.

·VII·

WHEN Etna basks and purrs,
Naples is more afraid
Than when she shows her Garnet Tooth;
Security is loud.

·VIII·

REVERSE cannot befall that fine Prosperity
Whose sources are interior.
As soon Adversity
A diamond overtake,
In far Bolivian ground;
Misfortune hath no implement
Could mar it, if it found.

·IX·

TO be alive is power,
Existence in itself,
Without a further function,
Omnipotence enough.

To be alive and Will —
'Tis able as a God!
The Further of ourselves be what —
Such being Finitude?

·X·

WITCHCRAFT has not a pedigree,
'Tis early as our breath,
And mourners meet it going out
The moment of our death.

·XI·

EXHILARATION is the Breeze
That lifts us from the ground,
And leaves us in another place
Whose statement is not found;
Returns us not, but after time
We soberly descend,
A little newer for the term
Upon enchanted ground.

·XII·

NO romance sold unto,
Could so enthrall a man
As the perusal of
His individual one.

'Tis fiction's to dilute
To plausibility
Our novel, when 'tis small enough
To credit, — 'tisn't true!

· XIII ·

IF what we could were what we would —
Criterion be small;
It is the Ultimate of talk
The impotence to tell.

· XIV ·

PERCEPTION of an
Object costs
Precise the Object's loss.
Perception in itself a gain
Replying to its price;
The Object Absolute is nought,
Perception sets it fair,
And then upbraids a Perfectness
That situates so far.

· XV ·

NO other can reduce
Our mortal consequence,
Like the remembering it be nought
A period from hence.
But contemplation for
Cotemporaneous nought
Our single competition;
Jehovah's estimate.

· XVI ·

THE blunder is to estimate, —
"Eternity is *Then*,"
We say, as of a station.
Meanwhile he is so near,
He joins me in my ramble,
Divides abode with me,
No friend have I that so persists
As this Eternity.

· XVII ·

MY Wheel is in the dark, —
I cannot see a spoke,
Yet know its dripping feet
Go round and round.

My foot is on the tide —
An unfrequented road,
Yet have all roads
A "clearing" at the end.

Some have resigned the loom,
Some in the busy tomb
Find quaint employ,
Some with new, stately feet
Pass royal through the gate,
Flinging the problem back at you and me.

· XVIII ·

THERE is another Loneliness
That many die without,
Not want or friend occasions it,
Or circumstance or lot.

But nature sometimes, sometimes thought,
And whoso it befall
Is richer than could be divulged
By mortal numeral.

·XIX·

SO gay a flower bereaved the mind
As if it were a woe,
Is Beauty an affliction, then?
Tradition ought to know.

·XX·

GLORY is that bright tragic thing,
That for an instant
Means Dominion,
Warms some poor name
That never felt the sun,
Gently replacing
In oblivion.

·XXI·

THE missing All prevented me
From missing minor things.
If nothing larger than a World's
Departure from a hinge,
Or Sun's extinction be observed,
'Twas not so large that I
Could lift my forehead from my work
For curiosity.

·XXII·

HIS mind, of man a secret makes,
I meet him with a start,
He carries a circumference
In which I have no part,
Or even if I deem I do —
He otherwise may know.
Impregnable to inquest,
However neighborly.

·XXIII·

THE suburbs of a secret
A strategist should keep,
Better than on a dream intrude
To scrutinize the sleep.

·XXIV·

THE difference between despair
And fear, is like the one
Between the instant of a wreck,
And when the wreck has been.

The mind is smooth, — no motion —
Contented as the eye
Upon the forehead of a Bust,
That knows it cannot see.

·XXV·

THERE is a solitude of space,
A solitude of sea,
A solitude of death, but these
Society shall be,

Compared with that profounder site,
That polar privacy,
A Soul admitted to Itself:
Finite Infinity.

·XXVI·

THE props assist the house
Until the house is built,
And then the props withdraw —
And adequate, erect,
The house supports itself;
Ceasing to recollect
The auger and the carpenter.
Just such a retrospect
Hath the perfected life,
A past of plank and nail,
And slowness, — then the scaffolds drop —
Affirming it a soul.

·XXVII·

THE gleam of an heroic act,
Such strange illumination —
The Possible's slow fuse is lit
By the Imagination!

·XXVIII·

TO disappear enhances;
The man who runs away
Is tinctured for an instant
With Immortality.

But yesterday a vagrant,
Today in memory lain
With superstitious merit
We tamper with again.

But never far as Honour
Removes the paltry One,
And impotent to cherish
We hasten to adorn.

Of Death the sharpest function,
That, just as we discern,
The Excellence defies us;
Securest gathered then

The fruit perverse to plucking,
But leaning to the sight
With the ecstatic limit
Of unobtained Delight.

· XXIX ·

DOWN Time's quaint stream
Without an oar,
We are enforced to sail,
Our Port — a secret —
Our Perchance — a gale.
What Skipper would
Incur the risk,
What Buccaneer would ride,
Without a surety from the wind
Or schedule of the tide?

· XXX ·

I BET with every Wind that blew, till Nature in chagrin
Employed a *Fact* to visit me and scuttle my Balloon!

·XXXI·

THE Future never spoke,
Nor will he, like the Dumb,
Reveal by sign or syllable
Of his profound To-come.
But when the news be ripe,
Presents it in the Act —
Forestalling preparation
Escape or substitute.
Indifferent to him
The Dower as the Doom,
His office but to execute
Fate's Telegram to him.

·XXXII·

TWO lengths has every day,
Its absolute extent —
And area superior
By hope or heaven lent.
Eternity will be
Velocity, or pause,
At fundamental signals
From fundamental laws.
To die, is not to go —
On doom's consummate chart
No territory new is staked,
Remain thou as thou art.

·XXXIII·

THE Soul's superior instants
Occur to Her alone,
When friend and earth's occasion
Have infinite withdrawn.

Or she, Herself, ascended
To too remote a height,
For lower recognition
Than Her Omnipotent.

This mortal abolition
Is seldom, but as fair
As Apparition — subject
To autocratic air.

Eternity's disclosure
To favorites, a few,
Of the Colossal substance
Of immortality.

·XXXIV·

NATURE is what we see,
The Hill, the Afternoon —
Squirrel, Eclipse, the Bumble-bee,
Nay — Nature is Heaven.

Nature is what we hear,
The Bobolink, the Sea —
Thunder, the Cricket —
Nay, — Nature is Harmony.

Nature is what we know
But have no art to say,
So impotent our wisdom is
To Her simplicity.

·XXXV·

AH, Teneriffe!
Receding Mountain!
Purple of Ages pause for you,
Sunset reviews her Sapphire Regiment,
Day drops you her red Adieu!

Still, clad in your mail of ices,
Thigh of granite and thew of steel —
Heedless, alike, of pomp or parting,
Ah, Teneriffe!
I'm kneeling still.

·XXXVI·

SHE died at play,
Gambolled away
Her lease of spotted hours,
Then sank as gaily as a Turk
Upon a couch of flowers.

Her ghost strolled softly o'er the hill
Yesterday and today,
Her vestments as the silver fleece,
Her countenance as spray.

·XXXVII·

"MORNING" means "Milking" to the Farmer
Dawn to the Apennines —
Dice to the Maid.
"Morning" means just Chance to the Lover —
Just Revelation to the Beloved.
Epicures date a breakfast by it!
Heroes a battle,
The Miller a flood,
Faint-going eyes their lapse
From sighing,
Faith, the Experiment of our Lord!

·XXXVIII·

A LITTLE madness in the Spring
Is wholesome even for the King,
But God be with the Clown,
Who ponders this tremendous scene —
This whole experiment of green,
As if it were his own!

·XXXIX·

I CAN'T tell you, but you feel it —
Nor can you tell me,
Saints with vanished slate and pencil
Solve our April day.

Sweeter than a vanished Frolic
From a vanished Green!
Swifter than the hoofs of Horsemen
Round a ledge of Dream!

Modest, let us walk among it,
With our "faces veiled",
As they say polite Archangels
Do, in meeting God.

Not for *me* to prate about it,
Not for *you* to say
To some fashionable Lady —
"Charming April Day!"

Rather Heaven's "Peter Parley"
By which, Children — slow —
To sublimer recitations
Are prepared to go!

·XL·

SOME Days retired from the rest
In soft distinction lie,
The Day that a companion came —
Or was obliged to die.

·XLI·

LIKE Men and Women shadows walk
Upon the hills today,
With here and there a mighty bow,
Or trailing courtesy
To Neighbors, doubtless, of their own;
Not quickened to perceive
Minuter landscape, as Ourselves
And Boroughs where we live.

·XLII·

THE butterfly obtains
But little sympathy,
Though favorably mentioned
In Entomology.
Because he travels freely
And wears a proper coat,
The circumspect are certain
That he is dissolute.
Had he the homely scutcheon of modest Industry,
'Twere fitter certifying for Immortality.

·XLIII·

BEAUTY crowds me till I die,
Beauty, mercy have on me!
But if I expire today,
Let it be in sight of thee.

· XLIV ·

WE spy the Forests and the Hills,
The tents to Nature's Show,
Mistake the outside for the in
And mention what we saw.

Could Commentators on the sign
Of Nature's Caravan
Obtain "admission", as a child,
Some Wednesday afternoon?

· XLV ·

I NEVER told the buried gold
Upon the hill that lies,
I saw the sun, his plunder done,
Crouch low to guard his prize.

He stood as near, as stood you here,
A pace had been between —
Did but a snake bisect the brake,
My life had forfeit been.

That was a wondrous booty,
I hope 'twas honest gained —
Those were the finest ingots
That ever kissed the spade.

Whether to keep the secret —
Whether to reveal —
Whether, while I ponder
Kidd may sudden sail —

Could a Shrewd advise me
We might e'en divide —
Should a Shrewd betray me —
"Atropos" decide!

XLVI

THE largest fire ever known
Occurs each afternoon,
Discovered is without surprise,
Proceeds without concern:
Consumes, and no report to men,
An Occidental town,
Rebuilt another morning
To be again burned down.

XLVII

BLOOM upon the Mountain, stated,
Blameless of a name.
Efflorescence of a Sunset —
Reproduced, the same.

Seed, had I, my purple sowing
Should endow the Day,
Not a tropic of the twilight
Show itself away.

Who for tilling, to the Mountain
Come, and disappear —
Whose be Her renown, or fading,
Witness, is not here.

While I state — the solemn petals
Far as North and East,
Far as South and West expanding,
Culminate in rest.

And the Mountain to the Evening
Fit His countenance,
Indicating by no muscle
The Experience.

·XLVIII·

MARCH is the month of expectation,
The things we do not know,
The Persons of prognostication
Are coming now.
We try to sham becoming firmness,
But pompous joy
Betrays us, as his first betrothal
Betrays a boy.

·XLIX·

THE Duties of the Wind are few —
To cast the Ships at sea,
Establish March,
The Floods escort,
And usher Liberty.

·L·

THE Winds drew off
Like hungry dogs
Defeated of a bone.
Through fissures in
Volcanic cloud
The yellow lightning shown.
The trees held up
Their mangled limbs
Like animals in pain,
When Nature falls
Upon herself,
Beware an Austrian!

· LI ·

I THINK that the root of the Wind is Water,
It would not sound so deep
Were it a firmamental product,
Airs no Oceans keep —
Mediterranean intonations,
To a Current's ear
There is a maritime conviction
In the atmosphere.

· LII ·

SO, from the mould,
Scarlet and gold
Many a Bulb will rise,
Hidden away cunningly
From sagacious eyes.
So, from cocoon
Many a Worm
Leap so Highland gay,
Peasants like me —
Peasants like thee,
Gaze perplexedly.

· LIII ·

THE long sigh of the Frog
Upon a Summer's day,
Enacts intoxication
Upon the revery.
But his receding swell
Substantiates a peace,
That makes the ear inordinate
For corporal release.

· LIV ·

A CAP of lead across the sky
Was tight and surly drawn,
We could not find the Mighty Face,
The figure was withdrawn.

A chill came up as from a shaft,
Our noon became a well,
A thunder storm combines the charms
Of Winter and of Hell.

· LV ·

I SEND two Sunsets —
Day and I in competition ran,
I finished two, and several stars,
While He was making one.

His own is ampler —
But, as I was saying to a friend,
Mine is the more convenient
To carry in the hand.

(Sent with brilliant flowers.)

· LVI ·

OF this is Day composed —
A morning and a noon,
A Revelry unspeakable
And then a gay Unknown;
Whose Pomps allure and spurn —
And dower and deprive,
And penury for glory
Remedilessly leave.

·LVII·

THE Hills erect their purple heads,
The Rivers lean to see —
Yet Man has not, of all the throng,
A curiosity.

·LVIII·

LIGHTLY stepped a yellow star
To its lofty place,
Loosed the Moon her silver hat
From her lustral face.
All of evening softly lit
As an astral hall —
"Father," I observed to Heaven,
"You are punctual."

·LIX·

THE Moon upon her fluent route
Defiant of a road,
The stars Etruscan argument,
Substantiate a God.
If Aims impel these Astral Ones,
The Ones allowed to know,
Know that which makes them as forgot
As Dawn forgets them now.

·LX·

LIKE some old-fashioned miracle
When Summertime is done,
Seems Summer's recollection
And the affairs of June.

As infinite tradition
As Cinderella's bays,
Or little John of Lincoln Green,
Or Bluebeard's galleries.

Her Bees have a fictitious hum,
Her Blossoms, like a dream,
Elate — until we almost weep
So plausible they seem.

Her Memories like strains — review —
When Orchestra is dumb,
The Violin in baize replaced
And Ear and Heaven numb.

·LXI·

GLOWING is her Bonnet,
Glowing is her Cheek,
Glowing is her Kirtle,
Yet she cannot speak!

Better, as the Daisy
From the Summer hill,
Vanish unrecorded
Save by tearful Rill,

Save by loving Sunrise
Looking for her face,
Save by feet unnumbered
Pausing at the place!

·LXII·

FOREVER cherished be the tree,
Whose apple Winter warm,
Enticed to breakfast from the sky
Two Gabriels yestermorn;

They registered in Nature's book
As Robin — Sire and Son,
But angels have that modest way
To screen them from renown.

·LXIII·

THE Ones that disappeared are back,
The Phoebe and the Crow,
Precisely as in March is heard
The curtness of the Jay —
Be this an Autumn or a Spring?
My wisdom loses way,
One side of me the nuts are ripe —
The other side is May.

·LXIV·

THOSE final Creatures, — who they are —
That, faithful to the close,
Administer her ecstasy,
But just the Summer knows.

·LXV·

SUMMER begins to have the look,
Peruser of enchanting Book
Reluctantly, but sure, perceives —
A gain upon the backward leaves.

Autumn begins to be inferred
By millinery of the cloud,
Or deeper color in the shawl
That wraps the everlasting hill.

The eye begins its avarice,
A meditation chastens speech,
Some Dyer of a distant tree
Resumes his gaudy industry.

Conclusion is the course of all,
Almost to be perennial,
And then elude stability
Recalls to immortality.

·LXVI·

A PROMPT, executive Bird is the Jay,
Bold as a Bailiff's hymn,
Brittle and brief in quality —
Warrant in every line;
Sitting a bough like a Brigadier,
Confident and straight,
Much is the mien
Of him in March
As a Magistrate.

·LXVII·

LIKE brooms of steel
The Snow and Wind
Had swept the Winter Street,
The House was hooked,
The Sun sent out
Faint Deputies of heat —
Where rode the Bird
The Silence tied
His ample, plodding Steed,
The Apple in the cellar snug
Was all the one that played.

·LXVIII·

THESE are the days that Reindeer love
And pranks the Northern star,
This is the Sun's objective
And Finland of the year.

·LXIX·

FOLLOW wise Orion
Till you lose your eye,
Dazzlingly decamping
He is just as high.

·LXX·

IN winter, in my room,
I came upon a worm,
Pink, lank, and warm.
But as he was a worm
And worms presume,
Not quite with him at home —
Secured him by a string
To something neighboring,
And went along.

A trifle afterward
A thing occurred,
I'd not believe it if I heard —
But state with creeping blood;
A snake, with mottles rare,
Surveyed my chamber floor,
In feature as the worm before,
But ringed with power.
The very string
With which I tied him, too,
When he was mean and new,
That string was there.

I shrank — "How fair you are!"
Propitiation's claw —
"Afraid," he hissed,
"Of me?"
"No cordiality?"
He fathomed me.
Then, to a rhythm slim
Secreted in his form,
As patterns swim,
Projected him.

That time I flew,
Both eyes his way,
Lest he pursue —
Nor ever ceased to run,
Till, in a distant town,
Towns on from mine —
I sat me down;
This was a dream.

·LXXI·

NOT any sunny tone
From any fervent zone
Finds entrance there.
Better a grave of Balm
Toward human nature's home,
And Robins near,
Than a stupendous Tomb
Proclaiming to the gloom
How dead we are.

·LXXII·

FOR Death, — or rather
For the things 'twill buy,
These put away

Life's opportunity.
The things that Death will buy
Are Room, — Escape
From Circumstances,
And a Name.
How gifts of Life
With Death's gifts may compare,
We know not —
For the rates stop Here.

·LXXIII·

DROPPED into the
Ether Acre!
Wearing the sod gown —
Bonnet of Everlasting laces —
Brooch frozen on!
Horses of blonde —
And coach of silver,
Baggage a strapped Pearl!
Journey of Down
And whip of Diamond —
Riding to meet the Earl!

·LXXIV·

THIS quiet Dust was Gentlemen and Ladies,
And Lads and Girls;
Was laughter and ability and sighing,
And frocks and curls.
This passive place a Summer's nimble mansion,
Where Bloom and Bees
Fulfilled their Oriental Circuit,
Then ceased like these.

·LXXV·

'TWAS comfort in her dying room
To hear the living clock,
A short relief to have the wind
Walk boldly up and knock,
Diversion from the dying theme
To hear the children play,
But wrong, the mere
That these could live, —
And This of ours must die!

·LXXVI·

TOO cold is this
To warm with sun,
Too stiff to bended be,
To joint this agate were a feat
Outstaring masonry.
How went the agile kernel out —
Contusion of the husk,
Nor rip, nor wrinkle indicate, —
But just an Asterisk.

·LXXVII·

I WATCHED her face to see which way
She took the awful news,
Whether she died before she heard —
Or in protracted bruise
Remained a few short years with us,
Each heavier than the last —
A further afternoon to fail,
As Flower at fall of Frost.

·LXXVIII·

TO-DAY or this noon
She dwelt so close,
I almost touched her;
Tonight she lies
Past neighborhood —
And bough and steeple —
Now past surmise.

·LXXIX·

I SEE thee better in the dark,
I do not need a light.
The love of thee a prism be
Excelling violet.

I see thee better for the years
That hunch themselves between,
The miner's lamp sufficient be
To nullify the mine.

And in the grave I see thee best —
Its little panels be
A-glow, all ruddy with the light
I held so high for thee!

What need of day to those whose dark
Hath so surpassing sun,
It deem it be continually
At the meridian?

·LXXX·

LOW at my problem bending,
Another problem comes,
Larger than mine, serener,
Involving statelier sums;

I check my busy pencil,
My ciphers slip away,
Wherefore, my baffled fingers,
Time Eternity?

·LXXXI·

IF pain for peace prepares,
Lo the "Augustan" years
Our feet await!

If Springs from Winter rise,
Can the Anemone's
Be reckoned up?

If night stands first, then noon,
To gird us for the sun,
What gaze —

When, from a thousand skies,
On our developed eyes
Noons blaze!

·LXXXII·

I FIT for them,
I seek the dark till I am thorough fit.
The labor is a solemn one,
With this sufficient sweet —
That abstinence as mine produce
A purer good for them,
If I succeed, —
If not, I had
The transport of the Aim.

·LXXXIII·

NOT one by Heaven defrauded stay,
Although He seem to steal,
He restitutes in some sweet way
Secreted in His will.

·LXXXIV·

THE feet of people walking home
In gayer sandals go,
The Crocus, till she rises,
The Vassal of the Snow —
The lips of Hallelujah!
Long years of practice bore,
Till bye and bye these Bargemen
Walked singing on the shore.

Pearls are the Diver's farthings
Extorted from the Sea,
Pinions the Seraph's wagon,
Pedestrians once, as we —
Night is the morning's canvas,
Larceny, legacy,
Death but our rapt attention
To immortality.

My figures fail to tell me
How far the village lies,
Whose Peasants are the angels,
Whose Cantons dot the skies,
My Classics veil their faces,
My Faith that dark adores,
Which from its solemn Abbeys
Such resurrection pours!

·LXXXV·

WE should not mind so small a flower,
Except it quiet bring
Our little garden that we lost
Back to the lawn again.
So spicy her Carnations red,
So drunken reel her Bees,
So silver steal a hundred Flutes
From out a hundred trees,
That whoso sees this little flower,
By faith may clear behold
The Bobolinks around the throne,
And Dandelions gold.

·LXXXVI·

TO the staunch Dust we safe commit thee;
Tongue if it hath, inviolate to thee —
Silence denote and Sanctity enforce thee,
Passenger of Infinity!

·LXXXVII·

HER "Last Poems" —
Poets ended,
Silver perished with her tongue,
Not on record bubbled other
Flute, or Woman, so divine;
Not unto its Summer morning
Robin uttered half the tune —
Gushed too free for the adoring,
From the Anglo-Florentine.
Late the praise —
'Tis dull conferring
On a Head too high to crown,

Diadem or Ducal showing,
Be its Grave sufficient sign.
Yet if we, no Poet's kinsman,
Suffocate with easy woe,
What and if ourself a Bridegroom,
Put Her down, in Italy?

(Written after the death of Mrs. Browning in 1861.)

·LXXXVIII·

IMMURED in Heaven! What a Cell!
Let every bondage be,
Thou Sweetest of the Universe,
Like that which ravished thee!

·LXXXIX·

I'M thinking on that other morn,
When Cerements let go,
And Creatures clad in Victory
Go up by two and two!

·XC·

THE overtakelessness of those
Who have accomplished Death,
Majestic is to me beyond
The majesties of Earth.

The soul her "not at Home"
Inscribes upon the flesh,
And takes her fair aerial gait
Beyond the hope of touch.

· XCI ·

THE Look of Thee, what is it like?
Hast thou a hand or foot,
Or mansion of Identity,
And what is thy Pursuit?

Thy fellows, — are they Realms or Themes?
Hast thou Delight or Fear
Or Longing, — and is that for us
Or values more severe?

Let change transfuse all other traits,
Enact all other blame,
But deign this least certificate —
That thou shalt be the same.

· XCII ·

THE Devil, had he fidelity,
Would be the finest friend —
Because he has ability,
But Devils cannot mend.
Perfidy is the virtue
That would he but resign, —
The Devil, so amended,
Were durably divine.

· XCIII ·

PAPA above!
Regard a Mouse
O'erpowered by the Cat;
Reserve within thy Kingdom
A "mansion" for the Rat!

Snug in seraphic cupboards
To nibble all the day,
While unsuspecting cycles
Wheel pompously away.

·XCIV·

NOT when we know
The Power accosts,
The garment of Surprise
Was all our timid Mother wore
At Home, in Paradise.

·XCV·

ELIJAH'S wagon knew no thill,
Was innocent of wheel,
Elijah's horses as unique
As was his vehicle.
Elijah's journey to portray,
Expire with him the skill,
Who justified Elijah,
In feats inscrutable.

·XCVI·

"REMEMBER me," implored the Thief—
Oh magnanimity!
"My Visitor in Paradise
I give thee Guaranty."

That courtesy will fair remain,
When the delight is dust,
With which we cite this mightiest case
Of compensated Trust.

Of All, we are allowed to hope,
But Affidavit stands
That this was due, where some, we fear,
Are unexpected friends.

·XCVII·

TO this apartment deep
No ribaldry may creep;
Untroubled this abode
By any man but God.

·XCVIII·

"SOWN in dishonor?"
Ah! Indeed!
May this dishonor be?
If I were half so fine myself,
I'd notice nobody!

"Sown in corruption?"
By no means!
Apostle is askew;
Corinthians 1:15, narrates
A circumstance or two!

·XCIX·

THROUGH lane it lay, through bramble,
Through clearing and through wood,
Banditti often passed us
Upon the lonely road.

The wolf came purring curious,
The owl looked puzzled down,
The serpent's satin figure
Glid stealthily along.

The tempest touched our garments,
The lightning's poignards gleamed,
Fierce from the crag above us
The hungry vulture screamed.

The satyr's fingers beckoned,
The valley murmured "Come" —
These were the mates — and this the road
Those children fluttered home.

· C ·

WHO is it seeks my pillow nights?
With plain inspecting face,
"Did you, or did you not?" to ask,
'Tis Conscience, childhood's nurse.

With martial hand she strokes the hair
Upon my wincing head,
"All rogues shall have their part in" —
What —
The Phosphorus of God.

· CI ·

HIS Cheek is his Biographer —
As long as he can blush,
Perdition is Opprobrium;
Past that, he sins in peace.
Thief

· CII ·

"HEAVENLY Father," take to Thee
The supreme iniquity,
Fashioned by Thy candid hand
In a moment contraband.

Though to trust us seem to us
More respectful — "we are dust."
We apologize to Thee
For Thine own Duplicity.

· CIII ·

THE sweets of Pillage can be known
To no one but the Thief,
Compassion for Integrity
Is his divinest Grief.

· CIV ·

THE Bible is an antique volume
Written by faded men,
At the suggestion of Holy Spectres —
Subjects — Bethlehem —
Eden — the ancient Homestead —
Satan — the Brigadier,
Judas — the great Defaulter,
David — the Troubadour.
Sin — a distinguished Precipice
Others must resist,
Boys that "believe"
Are very lonesome —
Other boys are "lost."
Had but the tale a warbling Teller
All the boys would come —
Orpheus' sermon captivated,
It did not condemn.

· CV ·

A LITTLE over Jordan,
As Genesis record,
An Angel and a Wrestler
Did wrestle long and hard.

Till, morning touching mountain,
And Jacob waxing strong,
The Angel begged permission
To breakfast and return.

"Not so," quoth wily Jacob,
And girt his loins anew,
"Until thou bless me, stranger!"
The which acceded to:

Light swung the silver fleeces
Peniel hills among,
And the astonished Wrestler
Found he had worsted God!

· CVI ·

DUST is the only secret,
Death the only one
You cannot find out all about
In his native town:
Nobody knew his father,
Never was a boy,
Hadn't any playmates
Or early history.

Industrious, laconic,
Punctual, sedate,
Bolder than a Brigand,
Swifter than a Fleet,
Builds like a bird too,
Christ robs the nest —
Robin after robin
Smuggled to rest!

·CVII·

AMBITION cannot find him,
Affection doesn't know
How many leagues of Nowhere
Lie between them now.
Yesterday undistinguished —
Eminent to-day,
For our mutual honor —
Immortality!

·CVIII·

EDEN is that old-fashioned House
We dwell in every day,
Without suspecting our abode
Until we drive away.
How fair, on looking back, the Day
We sauntered from the door,
Unconscious our returning
Discover it no more.

·CIX·

CANDOR, my tepid Friend,
Come not to play with me!
The Myrrhs and Mochas of the Mind
Are its Iniquity.

·CX·

SPEECH is a symptom of affection,
And Silence one,
The perfectest communication
Is heard of none —
Exists and its endorsement
Is had within —
Behold! said the Apostle,
Yet had not seen.

· CXI ·

WHO were "the Father and the Son" —
We pondered when a child,
And what had they to do with us —
And when portentous told
With inference appalling,
By Childhood fortified,
We thought, "at least they are no worse
Than they have been described."

Who are "the Father and the Son" —
Did we demand today,
"The Father and the Son" himself
Would doubtless specify,
But had they the felicity
When we desired to know,
We better Friends had been, perhaps,
Than time ensue to be.

We start, to learn that we believe
But once, entirely —
Belief, it does not fit so well
When altered frequently.
We blush, that Heaven if we achieve,
Event ineffable —
We shall have shunned, until ashamed
To own the Miracle.

· CXII ·

THAT Love is all there is,
Is all we know of Love;
It is enough, the freight should be
Proportioned to the groove.

·CXIII·

THE luxury to apprehend
The luxury 'twould be
To look at thee a single time,
An Epicure of me,
In whatsoever Presence, makes,
Till, for a further food
I scarcely recollect to starve,
So first am I supplied.
The luxury to meditate
The luxury it was
To banquet on thy Countenance,
A sumptuousness supplies
To plainer days,
Whose table, far as
Certainty can see,
Is laden with a single crumb —
The consciousness of Thee.

·CXIV·

THE Sea said "Come" to the Brook,
The Brook said "Let me grow!"
The Sea said "Then you will be a Sea —
I want a brook, Come now!"

·CXV·

ALL I may, if small,
Do it not display
Larger for its Totalness?
'Tis economy
To bestow a world
And withhold a star,
Utmost is munificence;
Less, though larger, Poor.

· CXVI ·

LOVE reckons by itself alone,
"As large as I" relate the Sun
To one who never felt it blaze,
Itself is all the like it has.

· CXVII ·

THE inundation of the Spring
Submerges every soul,
It sweeps the tenement away
But leaves the water whole.
In which the Soul, at first alarmed,
Seeks furtive for its shore,
But acclimated, gropes no more
For that Peninsular.

· CXVIII ·

NO Autumn's intercepting chill
Appalls this Tropic Breast,
But African exuberance
And Asiatic Rest.

· CXIX ·

VOLCANOES be in Sicily
And South America,
I judge from my geography.
Volcanoes nearer here,
A lava step, at any time,
Am I inclined to climb,
A crater I may contemplate,
Vesuvius at home.

·CXX·

DISTANCE is not the realm of Fox,
Nor by relay as Bird;
Abated, Distance is until
Thyself, Beloved!

·CXXI·

THE treason of an accent
Might vilify the Joy —
To breathe, — corrode the rapture
Of Sanctity to be.

·CXXII·

HOW destitute is he
Whose Gold is firm,
Who finds it every time,
The small stale sum —
When Love, with but a pence
Will so display,
As is a disrespect to India!

·CXXIII·

CRISIS is sweet and, set of Heart
Upon the hither side,
Has dowers of prospective
Surrendered by the Tried.
Inquire of the closing Rose
Which Rapture she preferred,
And she will tell you, sighing,
The transport of the Bud.

· CXXIV ·

TO tell the beauty would decrease,
To state the Spell demean,
There is a syllableless sea
Of which it is the sign.

My will endeavours for its word
And fails, but entertains
A rapture as of legacies —
Of introspective mines.

· CXXV ·

TO love thee, year by year,
May less appear
Than sacrifice and cease.
However, Dear,
Forever might be short
I thought, to show,
And so I pieced it with a flower now.

· CXXVI ·

I SHOWED her heights she never saw —
"Wouldst climb?" I said,
She said "Not so" —
"With me?" I said, "With me?"
I showed her secrets
Morning's nest,
The rope that Nights were put across —
And *now,* "Wouldst have me for a Guest?"
She could not find her yes —
And then, I brake my life, and Lo!
A light for her, did solemn glow,
The larger, as her face withdrew —
And could she, further, "No?"

·CXXVII·

ON my volcano grows the grass, —
A meditative spot,
An area for a bird to choose
Would be the general thought.

How red the fire reeks below,
How insecure the sod —
Did I disclose, would populate
With awe my solitude.

·CXXVIII·

IF I could tell how glad I was,
I should not be so glad,
But when I cannot make the Force
Nor mould it into word,
I know it is a sign
That new Dilemma be
From mathematics further off,
Than from Eternity.

·CXXIX·

HER Grace is all she has,
And that, so vast displays,
One Art, to recognize, must be,
Another Art to praise.

·CXXX·

NO matter where the Saints abide,
They make their circuit fair;
Behold how great a Firmament
Accompanies a star!

·CXXXI·

TO see her is a picture,
To hear her is a tune,
To know her an intemperance
As innocent as June;
By which to be undone
Is dearer than Redemption —
Which never to receive,
Makes mockery of melody
It might have been to live.

·CXXXII·

SO set its sun in thee,
What day is dark to me —
What distance far,
So I the ships may see
That touch how seldomly
Thy shore?

·CXXXIII·

HAD this one day not been,
Or could it cease to be —
How smitten, how superfluous
Were every other day!

Lest Love should value less
What Loss would value more,
Had it the stricken privilege —
It cherishes before.

·CXXXIV·

THAT she forgot me was the least,
I felt it second pain,
That I was worthy to forget
What most I thought upon.

Faithful, was all that I could boast,
But Constancy became,
To her, by her innominate,
A something like a shame.

·CXXXV·

THE incidents of Love
Are more than its Events,
Investments' best expositor
Is the minute per cents.

·CXXXVI·

A LITTLE overflowing word
That any hearing had inferred
For ardor or for tears,
Though generations pass away,
Traditions ripen and decay,
As eloquent appears.

·CXXXVII·

JUST so, Jesus raps — He does not weary —
Last at the knocker and first at the bell,
Then on divinest tiptoe standing
Might He out-spy the hiding soul.
When He retires, chilled and weary —
It will be ample time for me;
Patient, upon the steps, until then —
Heart, I am knocking low at Thee!

·CXXXVIII·

SAFE Despair it is that raves,
Agony is frugal,
Puts itself severe away
For its own perusal.

Garrisoned no Soul can be
In the front of Trouble,
Love is one, not aggregate,
Nor is Dying double.

·CXXXIX·

THE Face we choose to miss,
Be it but for a day —
As absent as a hundred years
When it has rode away.

·CXL·

OF so divine a loss
We enter but the gain,
Indemnity for loneliness
That such a bliss has been.

·CXLI·

THE healed Heart shows its shallow scar
With confidential moan,
Not mended by Mortality
Are fabrics truly torn.
To go its convalescent way
So shameless is to see,
More genuine were Perfidy
Than such Fidelity.

·CXLII·

GIVE little anguish
Lives will fret.
Give avalanches —
And they'll slant,

Straighten, look cautious for their breath,
But make no syllable —
Like Death,
  Who only shows his
  Marble disc —
Sublimer sort than speech.

·CXLIII·

TO pile like Thunder to its close,
Then crumble grand away,
While everything created hid —
This would be Poetry:
Or Love, — the two coeval came —
We both and neither prove,
Experience either, and consume —
For none see God and live.

·CXLIV·

THE Stars are old, that stood for me —
The West a little worn,
Yet newer glows the only Gold
I ever cared to earn —
Presuming on that lone result
Her infinite disdain,
But vanquished her with my defeat,
'Twas Victory was slain.

·CXLV·

ALL circumstances are the frame
In which His Face is set,
All Latitudes exist for His
Sufficient continent.

The light His Action and the dark
The Leisure of His Will,
In Him Existence serve, or set
A force illegible.

· CXLVI ·

I DID not reach thee,
But my feet slip nearer every day;
Three Rivers and a Hill to cross,
One Desert and a Sea —
I shall not count the journey one
When I am telling thee.

Two deserts — but the year is cold
So that will help the sand —
One desert crossed, the second one
Will feel as cool as land.
Sahara is too little price
To pay for thy Right hand!

The sea comes last. Step merry, feet!
So short have we to go
To play together we are prone,
But we must labor now,
The last shall be the lightest load
That we have had to draw.

The Sun goes crooked — that is night —
Before he makes the bend
We must have passed the middle sea,
Almost we wish the end
Were further off — too great it seems
So near the Whole to stand.

We step like plush, we stand like snow—
The waters murmur now,
Three rivers and the hill are passed,
Two deserts and the sea!
Now Death usurps my premium
And gets the look at Thee.

PART SIX

FURTHER POEMS

ONE

FITTER to see him I may be
For the long hindrance — grace to me
With Summers and with Winters grow,
Some passing year a trait bestow

To make me fairest of the earth.
The waiting then will seem so worth
I shall impute with half a pain
The blame that I was chosen then.

Time to anticipate his gaze —
Its first delight and then surprise,
The turning o'er and o'er my face
For evidence it be the grace
He left behind one day, so less,
He seek conviction that be this.

I only must not grow so new
That he'll mistake and ask for me
Of me, when first unto the door
I go, to elsewhere go no more.

I only must not change so fair
He'll sigh "the Real One where is she?"
The love though will array me right,
I shall be perfect in his sight.

If he perceive the other truth
Upon an excellenter youth,
How sweet I shall not lack in vain
But gain through loss, through grief obtain
The beauty that reward him best —
The beauty of Belief at rest.

(Now published for the first time 1930.)

· I ·

I FEAR a man of scanty speech,
I fear a silent man,
Haranguer I can overtake
Or babbler entertain —

But he who waiteth while the rest
Expend their inmost pound,
Of this Man I am wary —
I fear that He is Grand.

· II ·

PUBLICATION is the auction
Of the mind of man,
Poverty be justifying
For so foul a thing.

Possibly, — but we would rather
From our garret go
White unto the White Creator,
Than invest our snow.

Thought belongs to Him who gave it —
Then to him who bear
Its corporeal illustration.
Sell the Royal air
In the parcel, — be the merchant
Of the Heavenly Grace,
But reduce no human spirit
To disgrace of price!

· III ·

SOME work for Immortality,
The chiefer part for *Time;*
He compensates immediately,
The former checks on Fame.

Slow gold, but everlasting,
The bullion of To-day
Contrasted with the currency
Of Immortality.

A beggar here and there
Is gifted to discern
Beyond the broker's insight —
One's *Money* — One's the *Mine*.

· IV ·

THE popular Heart is a cannon first,
Subsequent a drum;
Bells for an auxiliary
And an afterward of rum.

Not a to-morrow to know its name,
Nor a past to stare,
Ditches for realms and a trip to jail
For a souvenir!

· V ·

FUNNY to be a Century
And see the people going by,
I should die of the oddity,
But then I'm not so staid as he.

He keeps his secrets safely, very —
Were he to tell, extremely sorry
This bashful globe of ours would be,
So dainty of publicity!

· VI ·

I CANNOT dance upon my toes,
No man instructed me,
But often times among my mind

A glee possesseth me
That had I ballet knowledge
Would put itself abroad
In pirouette to blanch a troupe,
Or lay a Prima mad!
And though I had no gown of gauze,
No ringlet to my hair,
Nor hopped for audiences like birds,
One claw upon the air, —
Nor tossed my shape in eider balls,
Nor rolled on wheels of snow
Till I was out of sight in sound,
The house encored me so —
Nor any knew I know the art
I mention easy here —
Nor any placard boast me,
It's full as opera!

·VII·

'TIS opposites entice,
Deformed men ponder grace,
Bright fires, the blanketless —
The lost, Day's face.

The blind esteem it be
Enough estate to see;
The captive strangles new
For deeming beggars play.

To lack enamour Thee,
Tho' the Divinity
Be only
Me.

· VIII ·

COLOR, Caste, Denomination —
These are Time's affair,
Death's diviner classifying
Does not know they are.

As in sleep — all here forgotten,
Tenets put behind,
Death's large democratic fingers
Rub away the brand.

If Circassian — He is careless —
If He put away
Chrysalis of Blonde or Umber,
Equal butterfly

They emerge from His obscuring;
What Death knows so well,
Our minuter intuitions
Deem incredible.

· IX ·

I RECKON, when I count at all,
First Poets — then the Sun —
Then Summer — then the Heaven of God —
And then the list is done.
But looking back — the first so seems
To comprehend the whole —
The others look a needless show,
So I write Poets — All.
This summer lasts a solid year,
They can afford a sun
The East would deem extravagant,
And if the final Heaven

Be beautiful as they disclose
To those who trust in them,
It is too difficult a grace
To justify the dream.

· X ·

THIS was a Poet — it is that
Distills amazing sense
From ordinary meanings,
And attars so immense
From the familiar species
That perished by the door,
We wonder it was not ourselves
Arrested it before.

Of pictures the discloser
The Poet, it is he,
Entitles us by contrast
To ceaseless poverty.

Of portion so unconscious
The robbing could not harm,
Himself, to him, a fortune
Exterior to Time.

· XI ·

STRONG draughts of their refreshing minds
To drink, enables mine
Through desert or the wilderness,
As bore it sealéd wine —
To go elastic, or as One
The camel's trait attained,
How powerful the stimulus
Of an hermetic mind!

· XII ·

WE miss a kinsman more
When warranted to see
Than when withheld by oceans
From possibility.

A furlong than a league
Inflicts a pricklier pain —
Till we, who smiled at Pyrenees,
Of parishes complain!

· XIII ·

WHO giants know, with lesser men
Are incomplete and shy,
For Greatness — that is ill at ease
In minor company.

A smaller could not be perturbed,
The summer gnat displays
Unconscious that his single sail
Does not comprise the sky.

· XIV ·

GROWTH of Man like growth of Nature
Gravitates within,
Atmosphere and sun confirm it
But it stirs alone.

Each its difficult ideal
Must achieve itself,
Through the solitary prowess
Of a silent life.

Effort is the sole condition,
Patience of itself —
Patience of opposing forces,
And distinct belief.

Looking on is the department
Of its audience,
But transaction is assisted
By no countenance.

· XV ·

DOOM is the House Without the Door —
'Tis entered from the sun,
And then the ladder's thrown away
Because escape is done.

'Tis varied by the dream
Of what they do outside,
When squirrels play and berries die —
And hundreds bow to God.

· XVI ·

EXPERIENCE is the angled road
Preferred against the mind
By paradox, the mind itself
Presuming it to lead
Quite opposite. How complicate
The discipline of man,
Compelling him to choose himself
His pre-appointed pain.

· XVII ·

I CAUTIOUS scanned my little life,
I winnowed what would fade
From what would last till heads like mine
Should be a-dreaming laid.

I put the latter in a barn,
The former blew away —
I went one winter morning,
And lo! my priceless hay

Was not upon the "scaffold",
Was not upon the "beam",
And from a thriving farmer
A cynic I became.

Whether a thief did it —
Whether it was the wind —
Whether Deity's guiltless
My business is to find.

So I begin to ransack —
How is it, Heart, with thee?
Art thou within the little barn
Love provided thee?

· XVIII ·

A BIRD is of all beings
The likest to the dawn,
An easy breeze does put afloat
The general Heavens upon.

It soars and shifts and whirls
And measures with the clouds
In easy, ever dazzling pace,
No different the birds —

Except a wake of music
Accompany their feet,
As should the Dawn emit a tune
For ecstasy of it.

· XIX ·

A PRISON gets to be a friend;
Between its ponderous face
And ours a kinsmanship exists,
And in its narrow eyes
We come to look with gratitude
For the appointed beam
It deals us — stated as our food,
And hungered for the same.

We learn to know the planks
That answer to our feet,
So miserable a sound at first
Nor even now so sweet
As plashing in the pools
When memory was a boy,
But a demurer circuit,
A geometric joy.

The posture of the key
That interrupts the day
To our endeavor, — not so real
The cheek of Liberty
As this companion steel,
Whose features day and night
Are present to us as our own
And as escapeless quite.

The narrow round, the stint,
The slow exchange of hope
For something passiver, — content
Too steep for looking up,
The liberty we knew
Avoided like a dream,
Too wide for any night but Heaven,
If that indeed redeem.

· XX ·

WHO court obtain
Within himself
Sees every man a king;
So poverty of monarchy
Is an interior thing.

No fate depose
Whom Fate ordain —
And who can add a crown
To him who doth continual
Repudiate his own?

· XXI ·

THE child's faith is new,
Whole — like his principle —
Wide — like the sunrise
On fresh eyes;
Never had a doubt,
Laughs at a scruple,
Believes all sham
But Paradise!

Audits the world —
Deems his dominion
Broadest of sovereignties,
And Caesar mean
By comparison,
Baseless emperor,
Ruler of naught,
Yet swaying all!

Grown by and by
To hold mistaken
His pretty estimate
Of prickly things,

He gains the skill
Sorrowful as certain,
Men to propitiate
Instead of *kings*.

·XXII·

FOREVER is composed of Nows —
'Tis not a different time,
Except for infiniteness
And latitude of home.

From this, experienced here,
Remove the dates to these,
Let months dissolve in further months,
And years exhale in years.

Without certificate or pause
Or celebrated days,
As infinite our years would be
As Anno Domini's.

·XXIII·

(*With a Daisy*)

A SCIENCE — so the savants say,
"Comparative Anatomy",
By which a single bone
Is made a secret to unfold
Of some rare tenant of the mold
Else perished in the stone.
So to the eye prospective led
This meekest flower of the mead,
Upon a winter's day,
Stands representative in gold
Of rose and lily, marigold
And countless butterfly!

· XXIV ·

TO offer brave assistance
To lives that stand alone
When one has failed to stop them
Is human, — but divine
To lend an ample sinew
Unto a *nameless* man,
Whose homely benediction
No other cared to earn.

· XXV ·

DRAMA'S vitalest expression
Is the Common Day
That arises, sets about us;
Other tragedy
Perish in the recitation,
This the more exert
When the audience is scattered,
And the boxes shut.

Hamlet to himself were Hamlet
Had not Shakespeare wrote,
Though the Romeo leave no record
Of his Juliet,
It were tenderer enacted
In the human heart —
Only theater recorded
Owner cannot shut.

· XXVI ·

A SECRET told
Ceases to be a secret then
A secret kept —
That can appal but one.

Better of it
Continual be afraid.
Than it and whom
You told it to, beside.

·XXVII·

I DWELL in Possibility,
A fairer house than Prose,
More numerous of windows,
Superior of doors.

Of chambers, as the cedars —
Impregnable of eye;
And for an everlasting roof
The gables of the sky.

Of visitors — the fairest —
For occupation — this —
The spreading wide my narrow hands
To gather Paradise.

·XXVIII·

EXPECTATION is contentment;
Gain, satiety.
But satiety, conviction
Of necessity.

Of an austere trait in pleasure.
Good, without alarm,
Is a too serene possession —
Danger deepens suns.

· XXIX ·

SHE dealt her pretty words like blades,
As glittering they shone,
And every one unbared a nerve
Or wantoned with a bone.

She never deemed she hurt,
That is not steel's affair;
A vulgar grimace in the flesh
How ill the creatures bear!

To ache is human, not polite;
The film upon the eye
Mortality's old custom —
Just locking up to die.

· XXX ·

REVOLUTION is the pod
Systems rattle from;
When the winds of Will are stirred,
Excellent is bloom.

But except its russet base
Every summer be
The entomber of itself,
So of Liberty.

Left inactive on the stalk,
All its purple fled,
Revolution shakes it
For test if it be dead.

·XXXI·

I'VE known a Heaven like a tent
To wrap its shining yards,
Pluck up its stakes and disappear
Without the sound of boards
Or rip of nail, or carpenter,
But just the miles of stare
That signalize a show's retreat
In North America.
No trace, no figment of the thing
That dazzled yesterday,
No ring, no marvel;
Men and feats
Dissolved as utterly
As birds' far navigation
Discloses just a hue;
A plash of oars — a gayety,
Then swallowed up to view.

·XXXII·

WE see comparatively.
The thing so towering high
We could not grasp its segment
Unaided yesterday,

This morning's finer verdict
Makes scarcely worth the toil —
A furrow our Cordillera,
Our Apennines a knoll.

·XXXIII·

A STILL volcano — Life —
That flickered in the night
When it was dark enough to show
Without endangering sight.

A quiet, earthquake style,
Too smoldering to suspect
By natures this side Naples.
The North cannot detect

The solemn, torrid symbol,
The lips that never lie,
Whose hissing corals part and shut
And cities slip away.

Therefore we do Life's labor
Tho' Life's reward be done —
With scrupulous exactness
To hold our senses on.

·XXXIV·

TO make routine a stimulus,
Remember it can cease —
Capacity to terminate
Is a specific grace.

PART SIX

FURTHER POEMS

TWO

· XXXV ·

IT'S easy to invent a life,
God does it every day —
Creation but a gambol
Of His authority.

It's easy to efface it,
The thrifty Deity
Could scarce afford eternity
To spontaneity.

The Perished Patterns murmur,
But His perturbless plan
Proceed — inserting here a Sun —
There — leaving out a Man.

· XXXVI ·

THE sweetest heresy received
That man and woman know,
Each other's convert —
Though the faith accommodate but two.

The churches are so frequent,
The ritual so small,
The Grace so unavoidable,
To fail — is infidel.

· XXXVII ·

I NEVER felt at home below,
And in the handsome skies
I shall not feel at home I know,
I don't like Paradise.

Because it's Sunday all the time
And recess never comes,
And Eden'll be so lonesome
Bright Wednesday afternoons.

If God could make a visit,
Or ever took a nap —
So not to see us — but they say
Himself a telescope

Perennial beholds us, —
Myself would run away
From Him and Holy Ghost and All —
But — there's the Judgment Day!

·XXXVIII·

OF course I prayed —
And did God care?
He cared as much
As on the air
A bird had stamped her foot
And cried "Give me!"

My reason, life
I had not had,
But for Yourself,
'Twere better charity
To leave me in
The atom's tomb,
Merry and nought
And gay and numb,
Than this smart misery.

·XXXIX·

I PRAYED at first — a little girl —
Because they told me to,
But stopped when qualified to guess
How prayer would sound to me

If I supposed God looked around
Each time my childish eye
Fixed full and steady on His own
In solemn honesty —

And told Him what I'd like to-day,
And parts of His far plan
That baffled me — the underside
Of His divinity.

And often since in danger
I count the force 'twould be
To have a God so strong as that,
To hold my life for me,

Till I could catch the balance
That slips so easily
It takes me all the while to poise,
And then it doesn't stay.

·XL·

IT always felt to me a wrong
To that old Moses done,
To let him see the Canaan
Without the entering.

And though in soberer moments
No Moses there can be,
I'm satisfied the romance
In point of injury

Surpasses sharper stated
Of Stephen or of Paul;
For these were only put to death,
While God's adroiter will

On Moses seemed to fasten
In tantalizing play —
As Boy should deal with lesser Boy
To show supremacy.

The fault was doubtless Israel's;
Myself had banned the Tribes,
And ushered grand old Moses
In pentateuchal robes

Upon the broad possession
But titled him to see.
Old Man on Nebo! Late as this
One Justice bleeds for thee!

· XLI ·

MY period had come for prayer,
No other art would do,
My tactics missed a rudiment;
Creator, was it you?

God grows above, so those who pray
Horizons must ascend,
And so I stood upon the North
To reach this curious Friend.

His house was not; no sign had He
By chimney nor by door, —
Could I infer His residence?
Wide prairies of the air

Unbroken by a settler,
Were all that I could see;
Infinitude, hadst Thou no face
That I might look on Thee?

The silence condescended,
The Heavens paused for me,
But awed beyond my errand
I worshiped — did not pray!

· XLII ·

WE pray to Heaven,
We prate of Heaven —
Relate when neighbors die,
At what o'clock to Heaven they fled.
Who saw them wherefore fly?

Is Heaven a place, and Sky a face?
Location's narrow way
Is for ourselves;
Unto the Dead
There's no geography.

· XLIII ·

"UNTO Me?"
"I do not know you —
Where may be your house?"

"I am Jesus — late of Judea,
Now of Paradise."

"Wagons have you to convey me?
This is far from thence" —

"Arms of mine sufficient phaeton,
Trust Omnipotence."

"I am spotted."
"I am Pardon."
"I am small."

"The least
Is esteemed in Heaven
The chiefest.
Occupy my house."

· XLIV ·

TOO much of proof affronts Belief, —
The Turtle will not try
Unless you leave him;
Then return —
And he has hauled away.

PART SIX

FURTHER POEMS

THREE

· XLV ·

THE Sun went down —
No man looked on,
The Earth and I alone
Were present at the majesty;
He triumphed and went on.

The Sun went up —
No man looked on,
The Earth and I and One —
A nameless bird, a stranger,
Were witness for the Crown.

· XLVI ·

THE tint I cannot take is best,
The color too remote
That I could show it in bazaar
A guinea at a sight —

The fine impalpable array
That swaggers on the eye
Like Cleopatra's company
Repeated in the sky —

The moments of dominion
That happen on the Soul
And leave it with a discontent
Too exquisite to tell —

The eager look on landscapes
As if they just repressed
Some secret that was pushing,
Like chariots, in the breast —

The pleading of the Summer,
That other prank of snow
That covers mystery with tulle
For fear the squirrels know —

Their graspless manners mock us,
Until the cheated eye
Shuts arrogantly in the grave,
Another way to see.

· XLVII ·

HEAVEN has different signs to me;
Sometimes I think that noon
Is but a symbol of the place,
And when again at dawn

A mighty look runs round the world
And settles in the hills,
An awe if it should be like that
Upon the ignorance steals.

The orchard when the sun is on,
The triumph of the birds
When they together victory make,
Some carnivals of clouds —

The rapture of concluded day
Returning to the West, —
All these remind us of the place
That men call "Paradise."

Itself a fairer we suppose,
But how ourself shall be
Adorned for a superior grace,
Not yet our eyes can see.

· XLVIII ·

THE rainbow never tells me
That gust and storm are by;
Yet is she more convincing
Than philosophy.

My flowers turn from forums,
Yet eloquent declare
What Cato couldn't prove to me
Except the birds were here!

· XLIX ·

BEAUTY is not caused, — it is:
Chase it and it ceases,
Chase it not and it abides,
Overtake the creases

In the meadow when the wind
Runs his fingers thro' it?
Deity will see to it
That you never do it.

· L ·

MY faith is larger than the hills,
So when the hills decay,
My faith must take the purple wheel
To show the Sun the way.

'Tis first he steps upon the vane
And then upon the hill;
And then abroad the world he goes
To do his golden will.

And if his yellow feet should miss,
The birds would not arise,
The flowers would slumber on their stems, —
No bells have Paradise.

How dare I therefore stint a faith
On which so vast depends,
Lest Firmament should fail for me —
The rivet in the bands.

·LI·

WITHIN my garden rides a bird
Upon a single wheel,
Whose spokes a dizzy music make
As 'twere a traveling mill.

He never stops, but slackens
Above the ripest rose,
Partakes without alighting,
And praises as he goes;

Till every spice is tasted,
And then his fairy gig
Reels in remoter atmospheres,
And I rejoin my dog.

And he and I perplex us
If positive 'twere we —
Or bore the garden in the brain
This curiosity?

But he, the best logician,
Refers my duller eye
To just vibrating blossoms —
An exquisite reply!

·LII·

THE Robin's my criterion of tune
Because I grow where robins do —
But were I Cuckoo born
I'd swear by him,
The ode familiar rules the morn.
The Buttercup's my whim for bloom
Because we're orchard-sprung —
But were I Britain-born
I'd daisies spurn —
None but the Nut October fits,
Because through dropping it
The seasons flit, I'm taught.
Without the snow's tableau
Winter were lie to me —
Because I see New Englandly.
The Queen discerns like me —
Provincially.

·LIII·

WE — Bee and I —
Live in the quaffing.
'Tisn't all hock with us,
Life has its ale —
But it's many a lay
Of the dim Burgundy
We chant for cheer
When the wines fail.
Do we "get drunk?"
Ask the jolly clovers!
Do we "beat our wife?"
I never wed.
Bee pledges *his* in minutest flagons
Dainty as the tress on her deft head.

While runs the Rhine
He and I revel —
First at the vat and
Latest at the vine;
Noon — our last cup —
"Found dead of nectar"
By a humming Coroner
In a by-thyme.

·LIV·

A FUZZY fellow without feet
Yet doth exceeding run!
Of velvet is his countenance
And his complexion dun.

Sometimes he dwelleth in the grass,
Sometimes upon a bough
From which he doth descend in plush
Upon the passer-by.

All this in summer —
But when winds alarm the forest folk,
He taketh damask residence
And struts in sewing silk.

Then, finer than a lady,
Emerges in the spring,
A feather on each shoulder —
You'd scarce accredit him.

By men yclept a caterpillar —
By me — but who am I
To tell the pretty secret
Of the Butterfly!

· LV ·

IF Nature smiles — the Mother must,
I'm sure, at many a whim
Of her eccentric family —
Is she so much to blame?

· LVI ·

TO intercept his yellow plan
The sun does not allow
Caprices of the atmosphere;
And even when the snow

Heaves balls of specks like vicious boy
Directly in his eye,
Does not so much as turn his head —
Busy with majesty!

'Tis his to stimulate the earth,
And magnetize the sea,
And bind astronomy in place —
Yet any passer-by

Would deem Ourselves the busier,
As the minutest bee
That rides supports a thunder,
A bomb to justify!

· LVII ·

BY my window have I for scenery
Just a sea with a stem —
If the bird and the farmer deem it a "Pine",
The opinion will serve for them.

It has no "Port", nor a "Line", but the jays
That split their route to the sky,
Or a squirrel whose giddy peninsular
May be easier gained this way.

For inlands the Earth is the underside,
And the upperside is the Sun,
And its commerce — if commerce it have —
Of spice, I infer from the odors borne.

Of its voice to affirm, when the wind is within,
Can the dumb divulge the Divine?
The definition of melody is
That definition is none.

It suggests to our faith, they suggest to our sight, —
When the latter is put away
I shall meet with conviction I somewhere met
That Immortality.

Was the Pine at my window a "Fellow"
Of the Royal Infinity?
Apprehensions are God's introductions
Extended inscrutably.

·LVIII·

OUT of sight? What of that?
See the bird reach it!
Curve on curve, sweep on sweep,
Round the steep air.
Danger! What is that to her?
Better 'tis to fail there
Than debate here.

Blue is blue the world through,
Amber, amber; dew, dew.
Seek friend, and see —
Heaven is sky of earth,
That's all —
Bashful Heaven, thy lovers small
Hide too, from thee.

· LIX ·

WHEN they come back,
If blossoms do —
I always feel a doubt
If blossoms can be born again
When once the art is out.

When they begin,
If Robins may —
I always had a fear
I did not tell, it was their last
Experiment last year.

When it is May,
If May return —
Had nobody a pang
Lest on a face so beautiful
He might not look again?

If I am there —
One does not know
What party one may be
To-morrow, — but if I *am* there
I take back all I say!

· LX ·

(*With Flowers*)

I'VE nothing else to bring, you know,
So I keep bringing these —
Just as the night keeps fetching stars
To our familiar eyes.
Maybe we shouldn't mind them
Unless they didn't come —
Then maybe it would puzzle us
To find our way home.

· LXI ·

I'M the little "Hearts' Ease!"
I don't care for pouting skies!
If the butterfly delay
Can I therefore stay away?

If the coward bumblebee
In his chimney-corner stay,
I must resoluter be;
Who'll apologize for me?

Dear old-fashioned little flower,
Eden is old-fashioned too!
Birds are antiquated fellows,
Heaven does not change her blue —
Nor may you, the little "Hearts' Ease",
Ever be induced to do.

· LXII ·

(*With a Flower*)

I PAY in satin cash —
You did not state your price,
A petal for a paragraph
Is near as I can guess.

·LXIII·

WHAT I can do — I will,
Though it be little as a Daffodil.
What I cannot, must be
Unknown to possibility.

·LXIV·

(Sent with a Flower)

DEFRAUDED I
A butterfly —
The lawful heir —
For thee.

·LXV·

COULD I do more for thee
Wert thou a bumblebee —
Since for the Queen have I
Nought but bouquet?

·LXVI·

THESE are the signs to Nature's inns,
Her invitation broad
For whomsoever famishing
To taste her mystic bread.

These are the rites of Nature's house,
The hospitality
That opens with an equal width
To beggar or to bee.

For sureties of her staunch estate,
Her undecaying cheer,
The purple in the East is set
And in the North, the star.

·LXVII·

SUNSET at night is natural,
But sunset in the dawn
Reverses Nature, Master,
So midnight's due at noon.

Eclipses be predicted
And Science bows them in,
But so one face us suddenly —
Jehovah's watch is wrong.

·LXVIII·

THROUGH the dark sod
As education,
The Lily passes sure,
Feels her white foot
No trepidation,
Her faith no fear.

Afterward in the meadow
Swinging her beryl bell,
The mold-life all forgotten now —
In ecstasy and dell.

·LXIX·

DELIGHT is as the flight,
Or in the ratio of it
As the schools would say.
The rainbow's way a skein
Flung colored after rain
Would suit as bright,
Except that flight were aliment.

"If it would last?"
I asked the East
When that bent stripe
Struck up my childish firmament,
And I for glee
Took rainbows as the common way,
And empty skies the eccentricity.

And so with lives,
And so with butterflies
Seen magic, through the fright
That they will cheat the sight
And dower latitudes far on
Some sudden morn,
Our portion in the fashion done.

· LXX ·

THE mountains grow unnoticed,
Their purple figures rise
Without attempt, exhaustion,
Assistance or applause.

In their eternal faces
The sun with broad delight
Looks long — and last — and golden,
For fellowship at night.

· LXXI ·

FOR every bird a nest,
Wherefore in timid quest
Some little wren goes seeking round?

Wherefore where boughs are free,
Households in every tree,
Pilgrim be found?

Perhaps a home too high —
The little wren desires.
Ah, aristocracy! —

The lark is not ashamed
To build upon the ground
Her modest house.

Yet who of all the throng
Dancing around the sun
Does so rejoice?

·LXXII·

(With a flower)

ALL the letters I can write
Are not fair as this,
Syllables of velvet,
Sentences of plush,
Depths of ruby, undrained,
Hid, lip, for thee —
Play it were a humming bird
And just sipped me!

·LXXIII·

MOST she touched me by her muteness;
Most she won me by the way
She presented her small figure —
Plea for charity.
Were a crumb my whole possession,
Were there famine in the land,
Were it my resource from starving,
Could I such a face withstand?
Not upon her knee to thank me
Sank this Beggar from the sky,
But the crumb partook, departed,
And returned on high

I supposed, when sudden —
Such a praise began,
'Twas as Space sat singing
To herself and Man.
'Twas the wingéd Beggar
Afterward I learned,
To her benefactor
Paying gratitude.

·LXXIV·

HOW many flowers fail in wood,
Or perish from the hill
Without the privilege to know
That they are beautiful!

How many cast a nameless pod
Upon the nearest breeze,
Unconscious of the scarlet freight
It bears to other eyes!

·LXXV·

AUTUMN overlooked my knitting;
"Dyes," said he, "have I
Could dishonor a flamingo."
"Give them me," said I.

Cochineal I chose for deeming
It resemble thee —
And the little border dusker —
That resembles me.

·LXXVI·

OH, Shadow on the Grass!
Art thou a step,
Or not?

Go make thee fair,
My candidate,
My nominated Heart!

Oh, Shadow on the Grass!
While I delayed
To guess,

Some other thou
Didst consecrate,
Oh, unelected face!

· LXXVII ·

THE last of summer is delight
Deterred by retrospect,
'Tis ecstasy's revealed review,
Enchantment's syndicate.

To meet it, nameless as it is,
Without celestial mail,
Audacious as without a knock
To walk within the vale.

· LXXVIII ·

CONJECTURING a climate
Of unsuspended suns
Gives poignancy to Winter;
The freezing fancy turns
To a fictitious country
To palliate a cold
Not obviated of degree
Nor eased of latitude.

PART SIX

FURTHER POEMS

FOUR

·LXXIX·

ALL but Death can be adjusted;
Dynasties repaired,
Systems settled in their sockets,
Centuries removed, —

Wastes of lives resown with colors
By supremer springs,
Death — unto itself exception —
Is exempt from change.

·LXXX·

HOW noteless men and Pleiads stand
Until a sudden sky
Reveals the fact that one is wrapt
Forever from the eye.

Members of the Invisible,
Existing while we stare
In leagueless opportunity
O'er-take-less as the air.

Why didn't we detain them?
The Heavens with a smile
Sweep by our disappointed heads,
But deign no syllable.

·LXXXI·

TO fill a gap —
Insert the thing that caused it.
Block it up
With other and 'twill yawn
The more;
You cannot solder an abyss
With air.

·LXXXII·

NOT any more to be lacked,
Not any more to be known —
Denizens of significance
For a span so worn —
Even Nature, Herself,
Has forgot it is there —
Too elate of her multitudes
To retain despair.

Of the ones that pursued it
Suing it not to go —
Some have solaced the longing
To accompany;
Some rescinded the wrench —
Others — shall I say?
Plated the residue of woe
With monotony.

·LXXXIII·

IT feels a shame to be alive
When men so brave are dead.
One envies the distinguished dust
Permitted such a head;

The stone that tells defending whom
This Spartan put away
What little of him we possessed
In pawn for liberty.

The price is great, sublimely paid,
Do we deserve a thing —
That lives, like dollars, must be piled
Before we may obtain?

Are we that wait sufficient worth,
That such enormous pearl
As Life should be dissolved for us
In battle's horrid bowl?

It may be a renown to live;
I think the men who die —
Those unsustained Saviors —
Present Divinity.

·LXXXIV·

THE doomed regard the sunrise
With different delight
Because when next it burns abroad
They doubt to witness it.

The man to die to-morrow
Detects the meadow bird,
Because its music stirs the axe
That clamors for his head.

Joyful to whom the sunrise
Precedes enamored day —
Joyful for whom the meadow bird
Has aught but elegy!

·LXXXV·

IT is dead. Find it —
Out of sound, out of sight.
"Happy?" Which is wiser,
You or the wind?
"Conscious?" Won't you ask that
Of the low ground?

"Homesick?" Many met it —
Even through them
This cannot testify —
Themselves dumb.

·LXXXVI·

MIDSUMMER was it when they died,
A full and perfect time;
The summer closed upon itself
In consummated bloom.

The corn her furthest kernel filled
Before the coming flail,
When these leaned into perfectness
Through haze of burial.

·LXXXVII·

THREE times we parted, Breath and I —
Three times He would not go
But stood to stir the flickering fan
The waters strove to stay.
Three times the billows tossed me up,
Then caught me like a ball,
Then made blue faces in *my* face
And pushed away a sail
That crawled leagues off, I liked to see
For thinking, while I die,
How pleasant to behold a thing
Where human faces be.
The waves grew sleepy, Breath did not,
The winds like children lulled,
The sunrise kissed my chrysalis —
And I stood up and lived.

·LXXXVIII·

WE talked as girls do, fond and late —
We speculated fair,
On every subject but the grave,
Of ours — none affair.

We handled destinies as cool
As we disposers be,
And God a quiet party
To our authority.

But fondest dwelt upon ourselves,
As we eventual be,
When girls to women softly raised,
We occupy Degree.

We parted with a contract
To recollect — and write —
But Heaven made both impossible
Before another night.

·LXXXIX·

'TWAS warm at first like us,
Until there crept thereon
A chill, like frost upon a glass,
Till all the scene be gone.

The forehead copied stone,
The fingers grew too cold
To ache, and like a skater's brook
The busy eyes congealed.

It straightened — that was all —
It crowded cold to cold —
It multiplied indifference
As Pride were all it could.

And even when with cords
'Twas lowered like a freight,
It made no signal, nor demurred,
But dropped like adamant.

· XC ·

THESE fair, fictitious people,
The women plucked away
From our familiar notice,
The men of ivory —

These boys and girls in canvas
Who dwell upon the wall
In everlasting childhood,
Where are they — can you tell?

Perhaps in places perfecter,
Inheriting delight
Beyond our small conjecture,
Our scanty estimate.

Remembering ourselves, we trust,
But blesseder than we,
Through knowing where we only hope —
Receiving — where we pray.

Of expectation also —
Anticipating us
With transport that would be a pain,
Except for Holiness —

Esteeming us, as exiles,
Themselves admitted home
Through gentle miracle of Death
The way ourselves must come.

· XCI ·

'TWAS the old road through pain,
That unfrequented one
With many a turn and thorn
That stops at Heaven.

This was the town she passed;
There, where she rested last,
Then stepped more fast,
The little tracks close pressed.

Then — not so swift,
Slow — slow —
As feet did weary go,
Then stopped — no other track.

Wait! Look! Her little book,
The leaf at love turned back,
The very hat,
And this worn shoe
Just fits the track —
Herself, though — fled.

Another bed, a short one
Women make to-night
In chambers bright,
Too out of sight, though,
For our hoarse Good Night
To touch her hand.

· XCII ·

DON'T put up my thread and needle,
I'll begin to sew
When the birds begin to whistle,
Better stitches so.

These were bent, my sight got crooked.
When my mind is plain
I'll do seams a Queen's endeavor
Would not blush to own.

Hems too fine for lady's tracing
To the sightless knot,
Tucks of dainty interspersion
Like a dotted dot.

Leave my needle in the furrow,
When I put it down —
I can make the zigzag stitches
Straight, when I am strong.

Till then, dreaming I am sewing,
Fetch the seam I missed
Closer, so I, at my sleeping,
Still surmise I stitch.

·XCIII·

OF nearness to her sundered things
The Soul has special times,
When Dimness looks the oddity,
Distinctness easy seems.

The shapes we buried dwell about
Familiar in the rooms,
Untarnished by the sepulchre
Our moldering playmate comes

In just the jacket that he wore,
Long buttoned in the mold,
Since we, old mornings, children played,
Divided by a world.

The grave yields back her robberies,
The years our pilfered things,
Bright knots of apparitions
Salute us with their wings —

As we it were that perished,
Themselves had just remained
Till we rejoin them, and 'twas They
And not Ourselves that mourned.

· XCIV ·

YOU'LL find it when you come to die
The easier to let go,
For recollecting such as went
You could not spare, you know.

And though their places somewhat filled —
As did their marble names
With moss — they never grew so full
You chose the newer times.

And when this world sets further back,
As dying say it does,
The former love distincter grows
And supersedes the fresh.

And thought of them so fair invites,
It looks too tawdry grace
To stay behind with just the toys
We bought to ease their place.

· XCV ·

LIFE is what we make it,
Death we do not know;
Christ's acquaintance with him
Justifies him, though.

He would trust no stranger,
Other could betray,
Just His own endorsement
That sufficeth me.

All the other distance
He hath traversed first,
No new mile remaineth
Far as Paradise.

His sure feet preceding,
Tender Pioneer —
Base must be the cowards
Dare not venture now.

· XCVI ·

WHY make it doubt — it hurts it so —
So sick to guess —
So strong to know —
So brave upon its little bed
To tell the very last they said
Unto Itself — and smile and shake
For that dear, distant, dangerous sake.
But, the Instead —
The pinching fear
That something it did do or dare
Offend the Vision, and it flee,
And They no more remember me
Nor ever turn to tell me why —
Oh, Master! this is misery!

· XCVII ·

HEAVEN is so far of the mind
That were the mind dissolved,
The site of it by architect
Could not again be proved.

'Tis vast as our capacity
As fair as our idea,
To him of adequate desire
No further 'tis than Here.

· XCVIII ·

THE world feels dusty
When we stop to die;
We want the dew then,
Honors taste dry.

Flags vex a dying face,
But the least fan
Stirred by a friend's hand
Cools like the rain.

Mine be the ministry
When thy thirst comes,
Dews of thyself to fetch
And holy balms.

· XCIX ·

IT'S coming — the postponeless Creature,
It gains the block and now it gains the door,
Chooses its latch from all the other fastenings,
Enters with a — "You know me, Sir?"
Simple salute and certain recognition,
Bold — were it enemy — brief were it friend,
Dresses each house in crêpe and icicle,
And carries one out of it to God.

· C ·

NO crowd that has occurred
Exhibit, I suppose,
The general attendance
That Resurrection does.

Circumference be full,
The long-subjected Grave
Assert his primogeniture,
The Dust adjust and live.

On atoms features place,
All multitudes that were
Efface in the comparison,
As suns annul a star.

Solemnity prevail,
Its individual doom
Possess each separate consciousness,
August, resistless, dumb.

What duplicate exist —
What parallel can be —
Of the stupendousness of this
To universe and me?

· CI ·

OVER and over, like a tune
The recollection plays,
Drums of the phantom battlements,
Cornets of Paradise!

Snatches from baptized generations,
Cadences too grand
But for the Justified processions
At the Lord's right hand.

PART SIX

FURTHER POEMS

FIVE

· CII ·

THE only news I know
Is bulletins all day
From Immortality.

The only shows I see
To-morrow and To-day,
Perchance Eternity.

The only One I meet
Is God, — the only street
Existence, this traversed

If other news there be,
Or admirabler show —
I'll tell it you.[1]

· CIII ·

THE soul's distinct connection
With immortality
Is best disclosed by danger,
Or quick calamity, —

As lightning on a landscape
Exhibits sheets of place
Not yet suspected but for flash
And bolt and suddenness.

· CIV ·

CONSCIOUS am I in my chamber
Of a shapeless friend,
He doth not attest by posture
Nor confirm by word.

[1] The first three lines of this poem occur in a letter to Colonel Higginson. See page 262 "Life and Letters of Emily Dickinson."

Neither place need I present him,
Fitter courtesy
Hospitable intuition
Of his company.

Presence is his furthest license,
Neither he to me
Nor myself to him by accent
Forfeit probity.

Weariness of him were quainter
Than monotony
Knew a particle of space's
Vast society.

Neither if he visit Other —
Does he dwell — or nay —
Know I, but instinct reports Him
Immortality.

· CV ·

PAIN expands the time,
Ages coil within
The minute circumference
Of a single brain.

Pain contracts the time
Occupied with shot,
Gamuts of eternities
Are as they were not.

· CVI ·

THE admirations
And contempts of time
Show justest through an open tomb —
The dying, as it were a height,

Reorganizes estimate,
And what we saw not
We distinguish clear,
And mostly see not
What we saw before.
'Tis compound vision —
Light enabling light —
The Finite furnished
With the Infinite —
Convex and concave witness,
Back toward time,
And forward toward
The God of Him.

· CVII ·

HAD I presumed to hope,
The loss had been to me
A value for the Greatness' sake,
As giants gone away.

Had I presumed to gain
A favor so remote,
The failure but confirm the Grace
In further Infinite.

'Tis failure not of Hope
But diligent Despair
Advancing on celestial lists
With faint terrestrial power.

'Tis Honor — though I die
For that no man obtain
Till he be justified by Death —
This is the second gain!

· CVIII ·

IT was not Saint,
It was too large —
Nor Snow —
It was too small.
It only held itself
Aloof —
Like something spiritual.

· CIX ·

MY soul accused me
And I quailed
As tongues of diamond
Had reviled.

All else accused me
And I smiled,
My soul that morning
Was my friend.

Her favor is the best disdain
Toward artifice of Time or men,
But her disdain — 'twere cooler bear
A finger of enameled fire!

· CX ·

ME from Myself to banish
Had I art,
Impregnable my fortress
Unto foreign heart.

But since Myself assault Me
How have I peace,
Except by subjugating
Consciousness?

And since We're mutual Monarch,
How this be
Except by abdication
Me — or Me?

·CXI·

ITS Hour with itself
The Spirit never shows;
What terror would enthrall the street
Could countenance disclose
The subterranean freight,
The cellars of the soul.
Thank God the loudest place He made
Is licensed to be still!

·CXII·

THE battle fought between the Soul
And No Man is the one
Of all the battles prevalent
By far the greater one.

No news of it is had abroad;
Its bodiless campaign
Establishes and terminates,
Invisible, Unknown.

Nor History record it,
As legions of a night
The sunrise scatters, — these endure,
Enact, and terminate.

·CXIII·

MY portion is defeat to-day,
A paler luck than victory,
Less paeans, fewer bells —
The drums don't follow me with tunes,
Defeat a something dumber means,
More difficult than bells.
'Tis populous with bone and stain,
And men too straight to bend again,
And piles of solid moan,
And chips of blank in boyish eyes,
And shreds of prayer and death's surprise
Stamped visible in stone.
There's something prouder over there —
The trumpets tell it in the air.
How different victory to him
Who has it, and the One
Who to have had it would have been
Contenteder to die.

·CXIV·

SUSPENSE is hostiler than Death.
Death, tho' soever broad,
Is just Death, and cannot increase —
Suspense does not conclude,
But perishes to live anew,
But just anew to die,
Annihilation plated fresh
With Immortality.

·CXV·

ON a columnar self
How ample to rely;
In tumult or extremity
How good the certainty

That lever cannot pry,
And wedge cannot divide
Conviction, that granitic base,
Though none be on our side.

Suffice us, for a crowd,
Ourselves — and rectitude —
And that companion not far off
From furthest good man —
God.

· CXVI ·

FAITH is the pierless bridge
Supporting what we see
Unto the scene that we do not,
Too slender for the eye.

It bears the soul as bold
As it were rocked in steel,
With arms of steel at either side
It joins behind the rail —

To what — could we presume —
The bridge would cease to be —
To our far vacillating feet
A first necessity.

· CXVII ·

THE lonesome for they know not what —
The Eastern exiles be,
Who strayed beyond the amber line
Some madder holiday.
And ever since the purple West
They strive to climb in vain —
As birds that tremble from the clouds
Do fumble at the strain

The blesséd ether taught them
Some transatlantic morn,
When heaven was too common to miss,
Too sure to dote upon.

·CXVIII·

INCONCEIVABLY solemn,
Things too gay
Pierce by the very press
Of imagery.

Their far parades
Halt on the eye
With a mute pomp,
A pleading pageantry.

Flags are a brave sight,
But no true eye
Ever went by one
Steadily.

Music's triumphant,
But a fine ear
Aches with delight
The drums to hear.

·CXIX·

I SHOULD not dare to be so sad
So many years again;
A load is first impossible
When we have put it down.
The Superhuman then withdraws,
And we who never saw
The Giant at the other side
Begin to perish now.

PART SIX

FURTHER POEMS

SIX

·CXX·

I TOOK one draught of life,
I'll tell you what I paid,
Precisely an existence —
The market price, they said.

They weighed me, dust by dust,
They balanced film with film,
Then handed me my being's worth —
A single dram of Heaven.

·CXXI·

SO the eyes accost and sunder
In an audience,
Stamped in instances forever,
So may countenance
Entertain without addressing
Countenance of One
In a neighboring horizon,
Gone as soon as known.

·CXXII·

IT was a quiet way
He asked if I was his.
I made no answer of the tongue
But answer of the eyes.

And then he bore me high
Before this mortal noise,
With swiftness as of chariots
And distance as of wheels.

The world did drop away
As countries from the feet
Of him that leaneth in balloon
Upon an ether street.

The gulf behind was not —
The continents were new.
Eternity it was — before
Eternity was due.

No seasons were to us —
It was not night nor noon,
For sunrise stopped upon the place
And fastened it in dawn.

·CXXIII·

THE Heart is the capital of the Mind,
The Mind is a single State.
The Heart and the Mind together make
A single continent.

One — is the population —
Numerous enough.
This ecstatic nation
Seek — it is Yourself.

·CXXIV·

I MAKE his crescent fill or lack,
His nature is at full
Or quarter — as I signify,
His tides do I control.

He holds superior in the sky
Or gropes at my command
Behind inferior clouds,
Or round a mist's slow colonnade.

But since we hold a mutual disc
And front a mutual day,
Which is the despot neither knows —
Nor whose the tyranny.

· CXXV ·

I CAME to buy a smile to-day,
But just a single smile,
The smallest one upon your cheek
Will suit me just as well,
The one that no one else would miss
It shone so very small —
I'm pleading at the counter, Sir,
Could you afford to sell?

I've diamonds on my fingers —
You know what diamonds are!
I've rubies like the evening blood,
And topaz like the star!

'Twould be a bargain for a Jew —
Say, may I have it, Sir?

· CXXVI ·

I TEND my flowers for thee,
Bright Absentee!
My fuchsia's coral seams
Rip, while the sower dreams.

Geraniums tint and spot,
Low daisies dot,
My cactus splits a beard
To show its throat.

Carnations tip their spice
And bees pick up.
A hyacinth I hid
Puts out a ruffled head,
And odors fall
From flasks so small
You marvel how they held.

Globe roses break
Their satin flake
Upon my garden floor,
Yet Thou not there —
I had as lief they bore
    No crimson more.
Thy flower be gay
Her Lord away!
It ill becometh me.
I'll dwell in calyx gray
How modestly, alway
Thy daisy,
Draped for Thee.

· CXXVII ·

ONE Life of so much consequence
That I for it would pay
My Soul's entire income
In ceaseless salary.
One pearl of such proportion
That I would instant dive
Although I *knew* to take it

Would cost me just a life.
The sea is full — I know it!
That does not blur my gem!
It burns distinct from all the row
Intact in diadem!
Oh, Life is thick — I know it!
Yet not so dense a crowd
But monarchs are perceptible
Far down the dustiest road!

·CXXVIII·

MY life had stood a loaded gun
In corners, till a day
The owner passed — identified,
And carried me away.

And now we roam the sov'reign woods,
And now we hunt the doe —
And every time I speak for him
The mountains straight reply.

And do I smile, such cordial light
Upon the valley glow —
It is as a Vesuvian face
Had let its pleasure through.

And when at night, our good day done,
I guard my master's head,
'Tis better than the eider duck's
Deep pillow to have shared.

To foe of his I'm deadly foe,
None stir the second time
On whom I lay a yellow eye
Or an emphatic thumb.

Though I than he may longer live,
He longer must than I,
For I have but the art to kill —
Without the power to die.

·CXXIX·

I CANNOT be ashamed
Because I cannot see
The love you offer;
Magnitude reverses modesty.

And I cannot be proud
Because a height so high
Involves Alpine requirements
And services of snow.

·CXXX·

LOVE, thou art high,
I cannot climb thee,
But, were it two,
Who knows but we,
Taking turns at the Chimbarazu,
Ducal at last, stand up by thee?

Love, thou art deep,
I cannot cross thee,
But were there two
Instead of one,
Rower and yacht some sov'reign summer,
Who knows but we'd reach the sun?

Love, thou art veiled,
A few behold thee --
Smile and alter,
Prattle and die.
Bliss were an oddity without thee,
Nicknamed by God Eternity.

· CXXXI ·

EMPTY my heart of thee —
Its single artery,
Begin to leave thee out —
Simply extinction's date.

Much billow hath the sea,
One Baltic — they.
Subtract thyself, in play,
And not enough of me
Is left to put away —
"Myself" meant thee.

Erase the root, no tree;
Thee — then no me —
The Heavens stripped,
Eternity's wide pocket picked.

· CXXXII ·

THE love a life can show below,
Is but a filament, I know,
Of that diviner thing
That faints upon the face of noon
And smites the tinder in the sun
And hinders Gabriel's wing.

'Tis this in music hints and sways,
And far abroad on Summer days
Distills uncertain pain.
'Tis this enamors in the East,
And tints the transit in the West
With harrowing iodine.

'Tis this invites, appals, endows,
Flits, glimmers, proves, dissolves,
Returns, suggests, convicts, enchants —
Then flings in Paradise!

·CXXXIII·

FOREVER at his side to walk
The smaller of the two,
Brain of his brain, blood of his blood,
Two lives, one Being, now.

Forever of his fate to taste,
If grief, the largest part —
If joy, to put my piece away
For that belovéd heart.

All life to know each other —
Whom we can never learn,
And by and by a change called "Heaven" —
Rapt neighborhood of men,
Just finding out what puzzled us
Without the lexicon!

·CXXXIV·

ALL forgot for recollecting
Just a paltry *One*.
All forsook for just a stranger's
New accompanying.

Grace of rank and grace of fortune
Less accounted than
An unknown content, possessing,
Estimate who can!

Home effaced, her faces dwindled,
Nature altered small —
Sun if shone — or storm if shattered,
Overlooked I all.

Dropped my fate, a timid pebble
In thy bolder sea,
Ask me, Sweet, if I regret it —
Prove myself of Thee.

·CXXXV·

WHAT would I give to see his face?
I'd give — I'd give my life of course,
But that is not enough!
Stop just a minute, let me think —
I'd give my biggest bobolink!
That makes two — him and life.
You know who June is?
I'd give her,
Roses a day from Zanzibar,
And lily tubes like wells;
Bees by the furlong,
Straits of blue

Navies of butterflies sailed through,
And dappled cowslip dells.
Then I have "shares"
In primrose "banks",
Daffodil "dowries," spicy "stocks,"
Dominions broad as dew,
Bags of doubloons adventurous bees
Brought me from firmamental seas,
And purple from Peru.
Now, have I bought it, Shylock? Say!
Sign me the bond!
I vow to pay
To him who pledges this —
One hour of her sov'reign's face!
Ecstatic contract!
Niggard grace!
My kingdom's worth of bliss!

· CXXXVI ·

THE sunrise runs for Both,
The East her purple troth
Keeps with the hill,
The noon unwinds her blue
Till one breadth cover Two
Remotest still.

Nor does the night forget
A lamp for each to set,
Wicks wide away,
The North her blazing sign
Enacts in iodine,
Till Both can see.

The midnight's dusky arms
Clasp hemispheres and homes,
And so upon her bosom One,
And One upon her hem,
Both lie.

·CXXXVII·

WHY do I love thee, Sir?
Because —
The wind does not
Require the grass
To answer wherefore, when
He pass,
She cannot keep her place.

The lightning never asked
An eye
Wherefore she shut
When he was by —
Because he knows
She cannot speak,
And reasons not contained
Of talk
There be — preferred by daintier folk.

·CXXXVIII·

WHERE Thou art — that is Home,
Cashmere or Calvary — the same,
Degree — or shame,
I scarce esteem location's name
So I may come.

What Thou do'st is delight,
Bondage as play be sweet,
Imprisonment content
And sentence sacrament,
Just we two meet!

Where Thou art not is Woe —
Though bands of spices blow,
What Thou do'st not — Despair —
Though Gabriel praise me, Sir!

·CXXXIX·

AH, necromancy sweet!
Ah, wizard erudite!
  Teach me the skill
That I instill the pain
Surgeons assuage in vain,
  Nor herb of all the plain
Can heal!

·CXL·

ONE and One are One,
Two be finished using,
Well enough for schools,
But for inner choosing,
Life — just, or Death —
Or the Everlasting.
Two would be too vast,
For the Soul's comprising.

·CXLI·

SOME say Good Night at night,
I say Good Night by day,
Good-by — the going utter me —

Good Night I still reply.
For parting — that is night
And presence simply dawn,
Itself the purple on the height
Denominated Morn.

· CXLII ·

I AM ashamed, I hide —
What right have I to be a bride,
So late a dowerless girl?
Nowhere to hide my dazzled face,
No one to teach me that new grace,
Nor introduce my soul.

Me to adorn how, tell —
Trinket to make me beautiful,
Fabrics of cashmere —
Never a gown of dun, more,
Raiment instead of Pompadour
For me, my soul, to wear.

Fingers to frame my round hair
Oval — as feudal ladies wore,
Far fashions fair,
Skill to hold my brow like an earl,
Plead like a whippoorwill,
Prove like a pearl.

Then for character
Fashion my spirit quaint,
While quick like a liquor,
Gay like Light
Bring me my best pride.
No more ashamed,

No more to hide,
Meek, let it be —
Too proud for pride,
Baptized this day
A Bride.

·CXLIII·

ALTHOUGH I put away his life,
An ornament too grand
For forehead low as mine to wear,
This might have been the hand

That sowed the flowers he preferred,
Or smoothed a homely pain —
Or pushed the pebble from his path,
Or played his chosen tune

On lute the least, the latest,
But just his ear could know
That what soe'er delighted it
I never would let go.

The foot to bear his errand,
A little boot I know
Would leap abroad like antelope
With just the grant to do.

His weariest commandment
A sweeter to obey
Than "Hide and Seek," or skip to flutes,
Or all day chase the bee.

Your servant, Sir, will weary,
The surgeon will not come,
The world will have its own to do,
The dust will vex your fame.

The cold will force your tightest door
Some February day,
But say my apron bring the sticks
To make your cottage gay,

That I may take that promise
To Paradise with me —
To teach the angels avarice
Your kiss first taught to me!

·CXLIV·

YOU see, I cannot see your lifetime,
I must guess
How many times it ache
For me today — confess

How many times for my far sake
The brave eyes film.
But I guess guessing hurts,
Mine get so dim!

Too vague the face
My own so patient covets,
Too far the strength
My timidness enfolds;

Haunting the heart
Like her transplanted faces,
Teasing the want
It only can suffice.

·CXLV·

I KNOW lives I could miss
Without misery,
Others — whose instant's wanting
Would be Eternity.

The last a scanty number,
'Twould scarcely fill a two,
The first — a gnat's horizon
Could easily outgrow.

· CXLVI ·

GOOD morning, Midnight!
I'm coming home,
Day got tired of me —
How could I of him?

Sunshine was a sweet place,
I liked to stay —
But Morn didn't want me — now —
So good night, Day!

I can look, can't I?
When the East is red?
The hills have a way, then,
That puts the heart abroad.

You are not so fair, Midnight —
I chose Day,
But please take a little Girl
He turned away!

· CXLVII ·

DENIAL is the only fact
Received by the denied,
Whose will, a blank intelligence
The day the Heaven died —
And all the Earth strove common round
Without delight or aim.
What comfort was it Wisdom was
The spoiler of our home?

·CXLVIII·

I HAD not minded walls
Were Universe one rock,
And far I heard his silver call
The other side the block.

I'd tunnel until my groove
Pushed sudden through to his,
Then my face take recompense —
The looking in his eyes.

But 'tis a single hair,
A filament, a law —
A cobweb wove in adamant,
A battlement of straw —

A limit like the veil
Unto the lady's face,
But every mesh a citadel
And dragons in the crease!

·CXLIX·

I ROSE because he sank —
I thought it would be opposite,
But when his power bent,
My Soul stood straight.
I told him Best must pass
Through this low arch of flesh;
No casque so brave
It spurn the grave —
I told him worlds I knew
Where monarchs grew
Who recollected us
If we were true.

And so with thews of hymn
And sinew from within,
In ways I knew not that
I knew, till then —
I lifted him.

·CL·

RENUNCIATION
Is a piercing virtue,
The letting go
A presence for an expectation —
Not now.

The putting out of eyes
Just sunrise,
Lest Day Day's great progenitor
Out-show.

Renunciation is the choosing
Against itself,
Itself to justify
Unto itself;
When larger function
Make that appear
Smaller, that sated vision
Here.

·CLI·

SO well that I can live without —
I love Thee;
Then how well is that?
As well as Jesus?
Prove it me
That He loved men
As I love Thee.

·CLII·

THE power to be true to you
Until upon my face
The Judgment push His picture,
Presumptuous of your place —
Of this — could man deprive me,
Himself the Heaven excel,
Whose invitation yours reduced
Until it shone too small.

·CLIII·

YOU taught me waiting with myself —
Appointment strictly kept,
You taught me fortitude of fate,
This also I have learnt.

An altitude of Death that could
No bitterer debar
Than Life had done before it,
Yet — there is a science more —
The Heaven *you* know to understand,
That you be not ashamed
Of me, in Christ's bright audience
Upon the further hand.

·CLIV·

LONGING is like the seed
That wrestles in the ground,
Believing if it intercede
It shall at length be found.

The hour and the zone
Each circumstance unknown,
What constancy must be achieved
Before it see the sun!

· CLV ·

ONLY a shrine
But mine;
I made the taper shine.
Madonna dim, to whom
All feet may come,
Regard a nun.
Thou knowest every woe,
Needless to tell Thee so,
But canst Thou do
The grace next to it —
Heal?
That looks a harder skill,
Still — just as easy, if it be
Thy will.
Grant me —
Thou knowest though,
So why tell Thee?

· CLVI ·

IF he were living — dare I ask?
And how if he were dead?
And so around the words I went
Of meeting them afraid.

I hinted changes, lapse of time,
The surfaces of years
I touched with caution, lest they slit
And show me to my fears.

Reverted to adjoining lives
Adroitly turning out
Wherever I suspected graves —
'Twas prudenter, I thought.

And He — I rushed with sudden force
In face of the suspense —
"Was buried" — "Buried!" He!
My life just holds the trench.

·CLVII·

WHY do they shut me out of Heaven?
Did I sing too loud?
But I can sing a little minor,
Timid as a bird.

Wouldn't the angels try me
Just once more?
Just see if I troubled them —
But don't shut the door!

Oh, if I were the gentlemen
In the white robes,
And they were the little hand that knocked —
Could I forbid?

·CLVIII·

AFTER great pain a formal feeling comes —
The nerves sit ceremonious like tombs;
The stiff Heart questions — was it He that bore?
And yesterday — or centuries before?

The feet mechanical
Go round a wooden way
Of ground or air or Ought, regardless grown,
A quartz contentment like a stone.

This is the hour of lead
Remembered if outlived,
As freezing persons recollect the snow —
First chill, then stupor, then the letting go.

·CLIX·

THERE is a languor of the life
More imminent than pain;
'Tis pain's successor, when the Soul
Has suffered all it can.

A drowsiness diffuses,
A dimness like a fog
Envelops consciousness
As mist obliterates a crag.

The surgeon does not blanch at pain,
His habit is severe,
But tell him that it ceased to feel —
The creature going there,

And he will tell you skill is late,
A mightier than he
Has ministered before him —
There's no vitality.

·CLX·

THERE is a pain so utter
It swallows Being up,
Then covers the abyss with trance
So memory can step
Around, across, upon it,
As One within a swoon
Goes steady, when an open eye
Would drop him bone by bone.

·CLXI·

JOY to have merited the pain
To merit the release;
Joy to have perished every step
To compass thee at last.

Pardon to look upon thy face
With these old-fashioned eyes —
Better than new could be, for that,
Tho' bought in Paradise —

Because they looked on thee before
And thou hadst looked on them —
Prove me, my hazel witnesses,
The features are the same.

So fleet thou wert when present,
So infinite when gone —
An Orient's apparition
Remanded of the morn.

The height I recollect
'Twas ever with the hills,
The depth upon my soul was notched
As floods on whites of wheels.

To haunt till Time has dropped
His slow decade away,
And haunting actualize to last
At least, Eternity.

·CLXII·

REHEARSAL to ourselves
Of a withdrawn delight
Affords a bliss like murder,
Omnipotent, acute.

We will not drop the dirk
Because we love the wound
The dirk commemorate,
Itself remind us that we died.

·CLXIII·

I TIE my hat, I crease my shawl,
Life's little duties do
Precisely as the very least
Were infinite to me.

I put new blossoms in the glass,
And throw the old away;
I push a petal from my gown
That anchored there, — I weigh

The time 'twill be till six o'clock,
I have so much to do —
And get existence some way back,
Stopped, struck, my ticking through.

We cannot put ourselves away
As a completed man
Or woman — when the errand's done
We came to flesh upon.

There may be miles on miles of nought
Of action, — sicker far,
To simulate is stinging work
To cover what we are

From science and from surgery,
Too telescopic eyes
To bear on us unshaded,
For their sake, not for ours.

·CLXIV·

WHEN I hoped, I recollect
Just the place I stood
In a chamber facing West —
Roughest air was good.

Not a sleet could bite me,
Not a frost could cool,
Hope it was that kept me warm —
Not merino shawl.

When I feared — I recollect
Just the day it was —
Worlds were swimming in the Sun,
Yet how Nature froze!

Icicles upon my soul
Prickled raw and cool,
Birds went praising everywhere,
Mine alone was still.

And the day that I despaired —
This if I forget,
Nature will that it be night
When the sun is set.

Dark shall overtake the hill,
Overtake the sky,
Nature hesitate before
Memory — and me.

· CLXV ·

FROM blank to blank
A threadless way
I pushed mechanic feet,
To stop or perish
Or advance —
Alike indifferent

If end I gained,
If ends beyond
Indefinite disclosed,
I shut my eyes
And groped as well,
'Twas lighter to be blind.

· CLXVI ·

I GOT so I could hear his name
Without —
Tremendous gain! —
That stop-sensation in my soul,
And thunder in the room.

I got so I could walk across
That angle in the floor
Where he turned — so — and I turned how —
And all our sinew tore.

I got so I could stir the box
In which his letters grew —
Without that forcing in my breath
As staples driven through.

Could dimly recollect a Grace —
I think they called it "God,"
Renowned to ease extremity
When formula had failed —

And shape my hands petition's way —
Tho' ignorant of word
That Ordination utters —
My business with the cloud.

If any Power behind it be
Not subject to despair,
To care in some remoter way
For so minute affair
As misery —
Itself too vast for interrupting more,
Supremer than —
Superior to —

· CLXVII ·

AT leisure is the Soul
That gets a staggering blow;
The width of Life before it spreads
Without a thing to do.

It begs you give it work,
But just the placing pins —
Or humblest patchwork children do,
To help its vacant hands.

· CLXVIII ·

"TILL death" is narrow loving;
The scantiest heart extant
Will hold you, till your privilege
Of finiteness be spent.

But he whose loss procures you
Such destitution that
Your life, too abject for itself,
Thenceforward imitate —

Until, resemblance perfect,
Yourself for his pursuit
Delight of nature abdicate,
Exhibit love somewhat.

·CLXIX·

AND this of all my hopes —
This is the silent end;
Bountiful colored my morning rose,
Early and sere its end.

Never bud from a stem
Stepped with so gay a foot,
Never a worm so confident
Bored at so brave a root.

·CLXX·

SAVIOR! I've no one else to tell
And so I trouble Thee,
I am the one forgot Thee so.
Dost Thou remember me?

Not for myself I came so far,
That were the little load —
I brought Thee the imperial heart
I had not strength to hold —

The heart I carried in my own,
Till mine too heavy be,
Yet strangest — *heavier* since it went —
Is it too large for Thee? [1]

·CLXXI·

IT ceased to hurt me, though so slow
I could not see the trouble go —
But only knew by looking back
That something had obscured the track.

[1] A short variant of this poem appears on page 150.

Nor when it altered, I could say —
For I had worn it every day
As constant as the childish frock
I hung upon the peg at night.

Nor what consoled it —
I could trace,
Except whereas 'twas wilderness
It's better, almost Peace.

·CLXXII·

A WIFE at daybreak I shall be;
Sunrise, hast thou a flag for me?
At midnight I am yet a maid —
How short it takes to make it bride!
Then, Midnight, I have passed from thee
Unto the East and Victory.

Midnight, "Good night!"
I hear them call.
The Angels bustle in the hall,
Softly my Future climbs the stair,
I fumble at my childhood's prayer —
So soon to be a child no more!
Eternity, I'm coming, Sir, —
Master, I've seen that face before.

·CLXXIII·

BEHIND me dips Eternity,
Before me Immortality,
Myself the term between —
Death but the drift of Eastern gray
Dissolving into dawn away
Before the West begins.

'Tis Kingdom — afterwards — they say,
In perfect pauseless monarchy,
Whose Prince is son of none —
Himself His dateless dynasty,
Himself Himself diversify
In duplicate divine.

'Tis Miracle before me then,
Then Miracle behind, between, —
A crescent is the sea
With midnight to the north of her
And midnight to the south of her,
And maelstrom in the sky.

·CLXXIV·

AS if the sea should part
And show a further sea —
And that a further, and the three
But a presumption be
Of periods of seas
Unvisited of shores —
Themselves the verge of seas to be —
Eternity is these.

·CLXXV·

NOT what we did shall be the test
When act and will are done,
But what our Lord infers we *would* —
Had we diviner been.

PART SEVEN

ADDITIONAL POEMS

(Published under the title, "Unpublished Poems")

ONE

· I ·

MY triumph lasted till the drums
Had left the Dead alone,
And then I dropped my victory
And, chastened, stole along

To where the finished faces
Conclusion turned on me —
And then I hated glory
And wished myself were They!

What is to be — is best descried
When it has also been, —
Could Prospect taste of Retrospect
The tyrannies of men

Were tenderer, diviner
The Transitive toward.
A bayonet's contrition
Is nothing to the Dead!

· II ·

MORE life went out, when He went,
Than ordinary breath,
Lit with a finer phosphor
Requiring in the quench

A power of renownéd cold —
The climate of the grave
A temperature just adequate
So anthracite to live.

For some an ampler zero,
A frost more needle keen
Is necessary to reduce
The Ethiop within.

Others extinguish easier —
A gnat's minutest fan
Sufficient to obliterate
A tract of citizen.

· III ·

SO much of Heaven has gone from Earth
That there must be a Heaven,
If only to enclose the saints
To affidavit given.

The missionary to the mole
Must prove there is a sky!
Location doubtless he would urge —
But what excuse have I?

· IV ·

HE fought like those who've nought to lose;
Bestowed himself to balls
As one who for a further life
Had not a further use!

Invited Death with bold attempt;
But Death was coy of him
As other men were coy of Death!
To him, to live was doom.

His comrades shifted like the flakes
When gusts reverse the snow;
But he remained alive because
Of vehemence to die!

· V ·

DID you ever stand in a cavern's mouth —
Widths out of the sun —
And look and shudder and block your breath
And deem to be alone
In such a place what horror,
How goblin it would be?
And fly as 'twere pursuing you? —
Then Loneliness looks so.

Did you ever look in a cannon's face
Between whose yellow eye
And yours the Judgement intervened,
The question of "to die"
Extemporizing in your ear
Distinct as satyrs' drums?
If you remember, and were saved,
It's liker *so,* it seems.

· VI ·

HE gave away his life —
To us gigantic sum! —
A trifle in his own esteem,
But magnified by fame

Until it burst the hearts
That fancied they could hold,
When quick it slipped its limit
And on the Heavens unrolled.

'Tis ours to wince and weep —
And wonder — and decay
By blossom's gradual process;
He chose maturity! —

And ripening, as we sowed,
Just obviated bud;
And when we turned to note the growth,
Broke perfect from the pod.

·VII·

UNTO like story trouble has enticed me —
How kinsmen fell,
Brothers and sisters who preferred the glory
And their young will
Bent to the scaffold, or in dungeons chanted
Till God's full time —
When they let go the ignominy, smiling,
And shame went still.

Unto guessed crests my moaning fancy lures me.
Worn fair
By heads rejected in the lower country;
Of honors there
Such spirit makes perpetual mention
That I, grown cold,
Step martial at my crucifixion
As trumpets rolled.

Feet small as mine have marched in revolution
Firm to the drum;
Hands not so stout hoisted them in witness
When speech went numb.
Let me not shame their sublime deportments
Drilled bright —
Beckoning Etruscan invitation
Toward Light!

·VIII·

IF any sink, assure that this now standing
Failed like themselves and, conscious that it rose,
Grew by the fact — and not the understanding
How weakness passed or force arose.

Tell that the Worst is easy in a moment,
Dread — but the whizzing before the ball;
When the ball enters, enters silence —
Dying annuls the power to kill.

·IX·

A TOOTH upon our peace
The peace cannot deface.
Then wherefore be the tooth?
To vitalize the Grace.

The Heaven hath a Hell
Itself to signalize,
And every sign before the place
Is gilt with sacrifice.

·X·

IF your Nerve deny you,
Go above your Nerve, —
You can lean against the Grave
If he fear to swerve.

That's a steady posture —
Never any bend
Held of those brass arms,
Best Giant made.

If your Soul see-saw,
Lift the Flesh door, —
The Poltroon wants oxygen —
Nothing more.

·XI·

THE first Day's Night had come—
And, grateful that a thing
So terrible had been endured,
I told my Soul to sing.

She said her strings were snapt,
Her bow to atoms blown;
And so, to mend her, gave me work
Until another morn.

And then a Day as huge
As Yesterday in pairs
Unrolled its horror on my face—
Until it blocked my eyes.

·XII·

SOMEHOW myself survived the night
And entered with the day;
That it be saved—the saved suffice
Without the formula.

Henceforth I take my living place
As one commuted, led
A candidate for morning chance—
But dated with the Dead.

·XIII·

TO whom the mornings stand for nights,
What must the midnights be!

· XIV ·

WE grow accustomed to the dark
When light is put away,
As when the neighbor hold the lamp
To witness her good-by

A moment we uncertain step
For newness of the night,
Then fit our vision to the dark
And meet the road, erect!

And so of larger darknesses —
Those evenings of the brain
When not a moon disclose a sign,
Or star come out, within.

The bravest grope a little
And sometimes hit a tree
Directly in the forehead, —
But, as they learn to see,

Either the darkness alters —
Or something in the sight
Adjusts itself to midnight —
And life steps almost straight.

· XV ·

THE lamp burns sure, within,
Tho' serfs supply the oil, —
It matters not the busy wick
At her phosphoric toil!

The slave forgets to fill —
The lamp burns golden on,
Unconscious that the oil is out
As that the slave is gone!

· XVI ·

A WEIGHT, with needles in the pounds
To push and pierce besides —
That if the flesh resist the heft,
The puncture coolly tries —

That not a pore be overlooked
Of all this compound frame;
As manifold for anguish
As spices be for name.

· XVII ·

I AM afraid to own a body,
I am afraid to own a soul;
Profound, precarious property,
Possession not optional.

Double estate entailed at pleasure
Upon an unsuspecting heir;
Duke in a moment of deathlessness,
And God for a frontier.

· XVIII ·

DID our Best Moment last
'Twould supersede the Heaven.
A few, — and they by risk, — procure,
So this sort are not given

Except as stimulants
In cases of despair
Or stupor. The reserve
These heavenly moments are —

A grant of the Divine —
That certain as it comes,
Withdraws, and leaves the dazzled Soul
In her unfurnished room.

· XIX ·

EXHILARATION is Within —
There can no Outer wine
So royally intoxicate
As that diviner brand

The Soul achieves, Herself,
To drink, or set away
For Visitor or Sacrament —
'Tis not of holiday.

To stimulate a Man
Who hath the ample Rhine
Within his closet, best you can
Exhale in offering.

· XX ·

BOUND a trouble and lives will bear it, —
Circumscription enable woe;
Still to conjecture were no limit,
Who were sufficient to misery?

State it the ages to a cypher
And it will ache contented on —
Sing at its pain, like any workman,
Notching the fall of the even Sun.

·XXI·

I SAW no way, the Heavens were stitched,
I felt the columns close;
The Earth reversed her hemispheres,
I touched the Universe

And back it slid — and I alone,
A speck upon a ball,
Went out upon Circumference —
Beyond the dip of bell!

·XXII·

WHAT twigs we held by! Oh the view
When, life's swift river striven through,
We pause before a further plunge
To take momentum! As the fringe
Upon a former garment shows
The garment cast, our props disclose
So scant, so eminently small,
Of might to help so pitiful,
To sink if we had labored fond
The diligence were not more blind.

How scant by everlasting light
The discs that satisfied our sight!
How dimmer than a Saturn's bar
The things esteemed for things that are!

·XXIII·

MUST be a woe,
A loss or so
To bend the eye
Best beauty's way.

But once aslant,
It gains delight
As clarified
As stalactite.

A common bliss
Were had for less,
The price — is
Even as the Grace.

Our Lord thought no
Extravagance
To pay — a Cross!

· XXIV ·

THE Martyr Poets did not tell,
But wrought their pang in syllable, —
That when their mortal fame be numb
Their mortal fate encourage some.

The Martyr Painters never spoke,
Bequeathing rather to their work, —
That when their conscious fingers cease
Some seek in Art the Art of Peace.

· XXV ·

FOR this accepted Breath,
Through it compete with Death,
The fellow cannot touch this Crown!
By it my title take,
Ah! what a royal sake
To my necessity stooped down!

No wilderness can be
Where this attendeth me;
No desert noon,
No fear of frost to come
Haunt the perennial bloom,
But certain June!

Get Gabriel to tell
The royal syllable;
Get Saints with new unsteady tongue
To say what trance below
Most like their glory show —
Fittest the Crown!

The second stanza (with a slight variant) was sent to Samuel Bowles about 1864. See "The Life and Letters of Emily Dickinson", Martha Dickinson Bianchi, Houghton Mifflin; p. 254.

PART SEVEN

ADDITIONAL POEMS

(Published under the title, "Unpublished Poems")

TWO

·XXVI·

TIME feels so vast
That were it not for an Eternity,
I fear me this Circumference
Engross my Finity

To His exclusion,
Who prepares by rudiments of size
For the stupendous volume
Of his Diameters.

·XXVII·

I SHALL keep singing! Birds will pass me
On their way to yellower climes;
Each with a robin's expectation, —
I with my redbreast and my rhymes.

Late — when I take my place in Summer,
But I shall sing a fuller tune;
Vespers are sweeter than Matins, Signor, —
Morning, only the seed of Noon.

·XXVIII·

IT'S thoughts and just one heart
And old sunshine about
Make frugal one's content —
And two or three for company
Upon a holiday
Crowded as Sacrament.

Books — when the unit
Spare the tenant long eno' —
A picture, if it care,

Itself a gallery too rare
For needing more;
Flowers to keep the eyes
From going awkward when it snows;
A bird, if they prefer,
Though Winter fire sing clear as plover
To our ear;
A landscape, not so great
To suffocate the eye;
A hill perhaps,
Perhaps the profile of a mill
Turned by the wind —
Though such are luxuries.

It's thoughts and just one heart
And Heaven about —
At least a counterfeit
We would not have correct —
And Immortality can be
Almost —
Not quite — content.

· XXIX ·

THEY shut me up in prose —
As when, a little girl,
They put me in the closet
Because they liked me "still."

"Still!" Could themselves have peeped
And seen my brain go round,
They might as wise have lodged a bird
For treason in the pound!

Himself has but to will,
And, easy as a star,
Look down upon captivity
And laugh. Nor more have I!

· XXX ·

I'M saying every day
"If I should be a Queen tomorrow
I'd do this way," —
And so I deck a little
If it be I wake a Bourbon
None on me bend supercilious
With "This was she
Begged in the market place
Yesterday."
Court is a stately place
I've heard men say,
So I loop my apron against the majesty
With bright pins of buttercup —
That not too plain
Rank overtake me —
And perch my tongue
On twigs of singing, rather high,
But this might be my brief term
To qualify, —
Put from my simple speech
All plain word,
Take other accents
As such I heard —
Though but for the cricket, just,
And but for the bee
Not in all the meadow
One accost me.
Better be ready
Than did next morn
Meet me in Arragon
My old gown on,
And the surprised air
Rustics wear
Summoned unexpectedly
To Exeter.

·XXXI·

NEVER for society
One shall seek in vain
Who his own acquaintance
Cultivate. Of men
Wiser ear may weary,
But the man within
Never knew satiety,
Better entertain
Than could border ballad
Or Biscayan hymn;
Neither introduction
Need you unto him.

·XXXII·

I'VE heard an organ talk sometimes
In a cathedral aisle
And understood no word it said,
Yet held my breath the while

And risen up and gone away
A more Bernardine girl,
Yet knew not what was done to me
In that old hallowed aisle.

·XXXIII·

I THINK I was enchanted
When first, a little girl,
I read that Foreign Lady[1] —
The dark felt beautiful!

[1] Elizabeth Barrett Browning

And whether it was noon at night,
Or only heaven at noon,
For very lunacy of light
I had not power to tell.

The bees became as butterflies,
The butterflies as moons
Lit up the low inferior grass;
And just the common tunes

That Nature murmured to herself,
To keep herself in cheer,
I took for Giants practising
Titanic opera.

The days to mighty metres stept,
The homeliest adorned
As if unto a Jubilee
'Twere suddenly confirmed.

I could not have defined the change —
Conversion of the mind,
Like sanctifying in the Soul,
Is witnessed, not explained.

'Twas a divine insanity.
The sorrow to be sane
Should I again experience,
'Tis antidote to turn

To tomes of solid witchcraft.
Magicians be asleep,
But magic hath an element
Like Deity to keep!

· XXXIV ·

A MIEN to move a queen —
Half child, half heroine —

An Orleans in the eye
That puts its manner by
For humbler company
When none are near —
Even a tear
Its frequent visitor.
A bonnet like a duke —
And yet a wren's peruke
Were not so shy
Of goer-by —
And hands so slight
They would elate a sprite
With merriment.
A voice that alters — low —
And on the ear can go
Like set of snow,
Or shift supreme
As tone of realm
On subject's diadem —
Too small to fear,
Too distant to endear, —
And so men compromise
And just revere.

·XXXV·

THE Winters are so short
I'm hardly justified
In sending all the birds away,
And moving into pod

Myself, — for, scarcely settled,
The phoebes have begun,
And then it's time to strike my tent,
And open house, again.

It's mostly interruptions,
My Summer is despoiled
Because there was a Winter once —
And all the cattle starved.

And so there was a Deluge
And swept the World away, —
But Ararat's a legend now —
And no one credits Noah!

·XXXVI·

MY first well day, since many ill,
I asked to go abroad
And take the sunshine in my hands
And see the things in pod —

A'blossom just when I went in
To take my chance with Pain,
Uncertain if Myself — or He —
Should prove the strongest One.

The Summer deepened while we strove:
She put some flowers away
And redder cheeked ones in their stead —
A fond elusive way

To cheat herself it seemed she tried,
As if before a child
To fade tomorrow, rainbows held
The sepulchre could hide.

She dealt a fashion to the nut,
She tied the hoods to seeds,
She dropped bright scraps of tint about
And left Brazilian threads

On every shoulder that she met —
Then both her hands of haze
Put up to hide her panting grace
From our unfitted eyes.

My loss by sickness — was it loss?
Or that ethereal gain
One earns by measuring the Grave —
Then — measuring the Sun!

·XXXVII·

THE day undressed herself —
Her garter was of gold,
Her petticoat of purple,
Her dimities as old

Precisely as the world!
And yet the newest star
Unrolled upon the firmament
Be wrinkled much as her.

Too near to God to pray,
Too near to Heaven to fear,
The Lady of the Occident
Retired without a care.

Her candles so expire
The flickering be seen
On ball of mast in foreign port,
On Bosphorus and dome.

·XXXVIII·

A SLASH of Blue, a sweep of Gray!
Some Scarlet patches on the way
Compose an evening sky!

A little Purple slipped between,
Some Ruby trousers hurried on,
A wave of Gold, a Bank of Day, —
This just makes out the morning sky!

·XXXIX·

A VISITOR in March —
Who influences flowers
Till they are orderly as busts
And elegant as glass, —

Who visits in the night —
And just before the sun,
Concludes his glistening interview,
Caresses — and is gone.

But whom his fingers touched —
And where his feet have run —
And whatsoever mouth he kissed —
Is as it had not been!

(*Jack Frost*)

·XL·

HAVE any, like myself,
Investigating March,
New houses on the hills descried
And possibly a church

That were *not,* we are sure,
As lately as the snow,
And *are* today, — if we exist, —
Though how may this be so?

Have any, like myself,
Conjectured who may be
The occupants of these abodes
So easy to the sky

'Twould seem that God should be
The nearest Neighbor to,
And Heaven a convenient grace
For show, or company?

Have any, like myself,
Preserved the charm secure
By shunning carefully the place
All seasons of the year

Excepting March? — 'Tis then
My villages be seen,
And possibly a steeple,
Not afterward — by men.

· XLI ·

THE birds reported from the South
A news express to me;
A spicy charge, my little posts,
But I am deaf today.

The flowers appealed — a timid throng —
I re-enforced the door;
"Go, Blossom, to the bees," I said,
"And trouble me no more!"

The summer grace for notice strove,
Remote her best array;
The heart to stimulate the eye
Refused too utterly.

At length a mourned like myself,
She drew away austere
Her frosts to ponder, — then it was
I recollected her.

She suffered me, for I had mourned, —
I offered her no word;
My witness was the black I bore,
Her witness was the Dead.

Thence forward we together dwelt;
She never questioned me,
Nor I herself, — our compact
A wordless sympathy.

· XLII ·

AN ignorance a sunset
Confer upon the eye
Of territory, color,
Circumference, decay.

Its amber revelation
Exhilarate, debase, —
Omnipotence' inspection
Of our inferior face.

And when the solemn features
Confirm, in victory,
We start, as if detected
In Immortality.

· XLIII ·

THE trees, like tassels, hit and swung;
There seemed to rise a tune
From miniature creatures
Accompanying the Sun,

Far Psalteries of Summer,
Enamouring the ear
They never yet did satisfy —
Remotest when most near.

The Sun shone whole at intervals,
Then half, — then utter hid,
As if himself were optional
And had estates of clouds

Sufficient to enfold him
Eternally from view,
Except it were a whim of his
To let the orchards grow.

A bird sat careless on the fence;
One gossiped in the lane
On silver matters, charmed a snake
Just winding round a stone.

Bright flowers slit a calyx,
Or soared upon a stem
Like hindered flags, sweet hoisted,
With spices in the hem.

'Twas more I cannot mention.
How mean, to those that see,
Van Dyke's delineation
Of Nature's Summer day!

·XLIV·

I KNOW where wells grow — droughtless wells —
Deep dug for Summer days,
Where mosses go no more away,
And pebble safely plays.

They're made of fathoms and a belt,
A belt of jagged stone
Inlaid with emerald half way down,
And diamonds jumbled on.

They have no bucket, — were I rich
A bucket I would buy;
I'm often thirsty, but my lips
Are so high up, you see.

I read in an old-fashioned Book
That people "thirst no more";
The wells have buckets to them, there, —
It must mean that, I'm sure.

Shall we remember parching, then?
Those Waters sound so grand!
I think a little well like mine
Dearer to understand.

· XLV ·

WHEN diamonds are a legend,
And diadems a tale,
I brooch and earrings for myself
Do sow, and raise for sale.

And though I'm scarce accounted,
My art a Summer day
Had patrons; once it was a Queen,
And once a Butterfly!

· XLVI ·

"ANSWER, July! —
Where is the Bee —
Where is the Blush —
Where is the Hay?"

"Ah," said July,
"Where is the Seed —
Where is the Bud —
Where is the May? —
Answer Thee me!"

"Nay," said the May,
"Show me the Snow —
Show me the Bells —
Show me the Jay!"

Quibbled the Jay,
"Where be the Maize —
Where be the Haze —
Where be the Burr?"
"Here!" — said the Year.

· XLVII ·

HE parts himself like leaves,
And then he closes up, —
Then stands upon the bonnet
Of any Buttercup.

And then he runs against
And oversets a Rose,
And then does nothing, —
Then away upon a jiff he goes,

And dangles like a mote
Suspended in the Noon,
Uncertain to return Below
Or settle in the Moon.

What came of him at night,
The privilege to say
Be limited by ignorance
What came of him that day.

The Frost obtain the world,
In cabinets be shown
A Sepulchre of quaintest floss,
An Abbey — a Cocoon.

·XLVIII·

COCOON above! Cocoon below!
Stealthy Cocoon, why hide you so
What all the world suspect?
An hour, and gay on every tree
Your secret perched in ecstasy
Defies imprisonment!

An hour in Chrysalis to pass,
Then gay above receding grass
A Butterfly to go!
A moment to interrogate,
Then wiser than a "Surrogate"
The universe to know!

·XLIX

SOME such butterfly be seen
On Brazilian Pampas
Just at noon — no later,
Then sweet license closes.

Some such spice express and pass
Subject to your plucking —
As the stars you knew last night,
Foreigners, this morning.

·L·

MY garden, like the beach,
Denotes there be a sea that's Summer —
Such as these the pearls
She fetches such as me.

(*Sent with flowers*)

·LI·

THEMSELVES are all I have —
Myself a freckled be.
I thought you'd choose a velvet cheek
Or one of ivory.
Would you instead of me?

(*Sent with flowers*)

·LII·

THE Grace myself might not obtain
Confer upon my flower;
Refracted but a countenance,
For I inhabit her.

·LIII·

BUT little carmine hath her face,
Of emerald scant, her gown;
Her beauty is the love she doth,
Itself enable mine!

(*With a flower*)

· LIV ·

THIS bauble was preferred by bees —
By butterflies desired —
At heavenly hopeless distance
Of bird was justified —
Did Noon embellish in herself —
Was Summer to a score
Who only knew of Universe
It had created her.

· LV ·

THE Flower must not blame the Bee
That seeketh his felicity
Too often at her door, —
But teach the footman from Vevay
Mistress is "not at home" to say
To people, any more!

· LVI ·

SHE hideth her the last,
And is the first to rise;
Her night doth hardly recompense
The closing of her eyes.

She doth her purple work,
And putteth her away
In low apartments in the sod
As worthily as we.

To imitate her life
As possible would be
As brew from our obtuser mints
The julep of the Bee!

·LVII·

THE Himalah was known to stoop
Unto the daisy low,
Transported with compassion
That such a doll should grow,
When, tent by tent, her universe
Hung out its flags of snow.

·LVIII·

IN Ebon Box, when years have flown,
To reverently peer,
Wiping away the velvet dust
Summers have sprinkled there!

To hold a letter to the light —
Grown tawny now with time —
To con the faded syllables
That quickened us like wine!

Perhaps a flower's shrivelled cheek
Among its stores to find,
Plucked far away some morning
By gallant, mouldering hand!

A curl, perhaps, from foreheads
Our Constancy forget;
Perhaps an antique trinket
In vanished fashions set!

And then to lay them quiet back
And go about its care,
As if the little Ebon Box
Were none of our affair!

· LIX ·

I PLAY at riches to appease
The clamoring for gold;
It kept me from a thief, I think,
For often, over bold

With want and opportunity,
I might have done a sin
And been myself that distant thing —
An independent man!

But often as my lot displays
Too hungry to be borne,
I deem myself what I would be, —
And so much comforting

My poverty and I derive,
We question if the man
Who own, esteem the opulence
As we, who never can.

Should ever these exploring hands
Chance sovereign on a mine,
Or in the long uneven term
To win become their turn,

How fitter they will be for want
Enlightening so well!
I know not which — desire or grant —
Be wholly beautiful!

· LX ·

THE Outer from the Inner
Derives its magnitude;
'Tis duke or dwarf according
As is the central mood

The fine unvarying axis
That regulates the wheel,
Though spokes spin more conspicuous
And fling a dust the while.

The Inner paints the Outer;
The brush without the hand
Its picture publishes precise
As is the inner brand

On fine arterial canvas —
A cheek, perchance a brow.
The stars' whole secret in the lake
Eyes were not meant to know.

· L X I ·

SIZE circumscribes, it has no room
For petty furniture;
The Giant tolerates no Gnat
For ease of Gianture —

Repudiates it, all the more,
Because intrinsic size
Ignores the possibility
Of Calumnies or Flies.

· L X I I ·

MYSELF was formed a carpenter.
An unpretending time
My plans and I together wrought
Before a builder came

To measure our attainments —
Had we the Art of Boards
Sufficiently developed
He'd hire us at halves.

My tools took human faces,
The bench where we had toiled
Against the man persuaded.
"We temples build," I said.

·LXIII·

"HAD I not This — or This," I said,
Appealing to myself
In moment of prosperity,
"Inadequate were life."

"Thou hast not Me — or Me!" it said
In moment of reverse,
"And yet thou art industrious —
No need hadst thou of Us."

"My need was all I had," I said.
The need did not reduce;
Because the food exterminate
The hunger does not cease,

But diligence is sharper
Proportioned to the chance;
To feed upon the retrograde
Enfeebles the advance.

·LXIV·

REMOVED from accident of loss
By accident of gain
Befalling not my simple days,
Myself had just to earn.

Of riches as unconscious
As is the brown Malay
Of pearls in Eastern waters
Marked his. What holiday

Would stir his slow conception
Had he the power to dream
That but the dower's fraction
Awaited even — him!

· LXV ·

TRUST in the Unexpected!
By this was William Kidd
Persuaded of the buried gold,
As one had testified.

Through this the old philosopher
His Talismanic Stone
Discerned, — still withholden
To effort undivine.

'Twas this allured Columbus
When Genoa withdrew
Before an apparition
Baptized America.

The same afflicted Thomas
When Deity assured
'Twas better — the perceiving *not*,
Provided it believed!

· LXVI ·

UNFULFILLED to observation,
Incomplete to eye —
But to Faith a revelation
In locality —
Unto us the suns extinguish.
To our opposite
New horizons they replenish,
Fronting us with night.

·LXVII·

WE dream, — it is good we are dreaming,
It would hurt us were we awake;
But since it is playing kill us,
And we are playing shriek,

What harm? Men die externally,
It is a truth of Blood, —
But we are dying in Drama,
And Drama is never dead.

Cautions we give each other,
And seldom open the eyes
Lest the phantasm prove the mistake just,
And the livid surprise

Cool us to shafts of granite,
With just an age and name
And perhaps a Latin inscription.
It's prudenter to dream!

·LXVIII·

DREAMS are well, but waking's better
If one wakes at morn!
If one wake at midnight better
Dreaming of the dawn.

Sweeter the surmising robins
Never gladdened tree,
Than a solid dawn confronting,
Leading to no day.

·LXIX·

TO put this world down like a bundle
And steady walk away
Reqtuires energy — possibly agony;
'Tis the scarlet Way

Trodden with straight renunciation
By the Son of God;
Later, his faint confederates
Justify the Road.

Flavors of that old Crucifixion,
Filaments of bloom
Pontius Pilate sowed, — strong clusters
From Barrabas' tomb.

Sacraments Saints partook before us,
Patent — every drop —
With the Brand of the Gentile Drinker
Who indorsed the Cup.

·LXX·

I SOMETIMES drop it, for a quick,
The thought to be alive —
Anonymous delight to know
And madder to conceive

Consoles a woe so monstrous,
That did it tear all day
Without an instant's respite —
'Twould look too far to die.

Delirium diverts the wretch
For whom the scaffold neighs;
The hammock's motion lulls the heads
So close on Paradise.

A reef crawled easy from the sea
Eats off the brittle line;
The sailor doesn't know the stroke,
Until he's past the pain.

·LXXI·

A PLATED life diversified
With gold and silver pain
To prove the presence of the ore
In particles! 'Tis when
A nature struggle, it exist.
A power will proclaim,
Although annihilation pile
Whole chaoses on him!

PART SEVEN

ADDITIONAL POEMS

(Published under the Title, "Unpublished Poems")

THREE

·LXXII·

YOU'LL know it as you know 'tis Noon —
By Glory! As you do the Sun —
By Glory! As you will in Heaven
Know God the Father and the Son!

By intuition mightiest things
Assert themselves, and not by terms.
"I'm Midnight," need the Midnight say?
"I'm Sunrise," need the Majesty?

Omnipotence had not a tongue:
His lisp is Lightning and the Sun,
His conversation with the Sea.
"How shall you know?" Consult your eye!

·LXXIII·

A TRANSPORT one cannot contain
May yet a transport be,
Though God forbid it lift the lid
Unto its ecstasy!

A diagram of rapture
A sixpence at a show!
With Seraphim in cages
The Universe would go!

·LXXIV·

I THINK to live may be a bliss,
To those who dare to try,
Beyond my limit to conceive,
My lips to testify.

I think the heart I former wore
Could widen — till to me
The other, like the little bank
Appear unto the Sea.

I think the days could every one
In ordination stand,
And majesty be easier
Than an inferior kind.

No numb alarm lest difference come,
No goblin on the bloom,
No start in apprehension's ear,
No bankruptcy, no doom, —

But certainties of sun,
Mid-summer in the mind,
A steadfast south upon the soul,
Her polar time behind.

The vision, pondered long,
So plausible becomes
That I esteem the fiction real —
The real, fictitious seems.

How beautiful the dream!
What plenty it would be
Had all my life but been mistake
Just rectified by Thee!

· LXXV ·

THE Heaven vests for each
In that small Deity
It craved the grace to worship
Some bashful Summer's day,

Half shrinking from the glory
It importuned to see,
Till these faint tabernacles drop
In full eternity.

How imminent the venture —
As one should sue a star
For his mean sake to leave the row
And entertain despair!

A clemency so common
We almost cease to fear,
Enabling the minutest
And furthest to adore!

· LXXVI ·

YOU know that portrait in the moon,
So tell me who 'tis like —
The very brow, the stooping eyes
A-fog for — say, whose sake?

The very pattern of the cheek,
It varies in the chin, —
But Ishmael, since *we* met 'tis long —
And fashions intervene.

When morn's at full 'tis Thou, I say,
My lips just hold the name, —
When crescent — Thou art worn I note,
But there the golden same.

And when some night bold slashing clouds
Cut Thee away from me,
That's easier than the other film
That glazes holiday.

·LXXVII·

MANY a phrase has the English language, —
I have heard but one
Low as the laughter of the cricket,
Loud as the thunder's tongue;

Murmuring like old Caspian choirs
When the tide's a'lull,
Saying itself in new inflection
Like a whippoorwill;

Breaking in bright orthography
On my simple sleep;
Thundering its perspective
Till I stir and weep —

Not for the sorrow done me,
But for the push of joy;
Say it again — Saxon!
Hush — only to me!

·LXXVIII·

PROMISE this, when you be dying
Some shall summon me;
Mine belong your latest sighing,
Mine to belt your eye —

Not with coins, though they be minted
From an Emperor's hand;
Be my lips the only buckle
Your low eyes demand.

Mine to stay, when all have wandered,
To devise once more
If the life be too surrendered
Life of mine restore.

Poured like this, my whole libation,
Just that you should see
Bliss of Death Life's bliss surpass
In more resembling you.

Mine to guard your narrow precinct,
To entice the sun
Longest on your south to linger;
Regal dews of morn

To demand, in your low favor,
Lest the jealous grass
Greener lean, or fonder cluster
Round some other face.

Mine to supplicate Madonna,
If Madonna be
Could regard so scarce a creature, —
Christ omitted me.

Just to follow your dear features,
Ne'er so far behind,
For my Heaven, of all Her glories
Worthiest to have gained.

·LXXIX·

THAT first day when you praised me, Sweet,
And said that I was strong
And could be mighty, if I liked, —
That day, the days among,

Glows central, like a Jewel
Between diverging golds:
The minor one that gleamed behind,
And Master of the Worlds!

LXXX

NOT probable — the merest chance —
A smile too few — a word too much —
And far from Heaven as the rest
The soul so close on Paradise.

What if the bird from journey far,
Confused by sweets, as mortals are,
Forget the secret of his wing
And perish — but a bough between?
Oh groping feet — oh phantom Queen!

LXXXI

AH Moon and Star!
You are very far —
But were no one further than you,
Do you think I'd stop for a Firmament —
Or a Cubit — or so?

I could borrow a bonnet of the lark,
And a chamois' silver boot,
And a stirrup of an antelope,
And be with you — Tonight!

But, Moon and Star,
Though you're very far,
There is One — further than you, —
He is more than Firmament from me,
So I can never go!

LXXXII

I COULD suffice for Him, I knew,
He could suffice for me;
Yet hesitating Fractions, Both
Surveyed Infinity.

"Would I be whole?" He sudden broached.
My syllable rebelled;
'Twas face to face with Nature forced,
'Twas face to face with God.

Withdrew the Sun to other Wests,
Withdrew the furthest Star
Before Decision stooped to speech,
And then be audibler

The answer of the Sea unto
The motion of the Moon,
Herself adjust her tides unto, —
Could I do else with mine?

·LXXXIII·

THE day that I was crowned
Was like the other days,
Until the Coronation came —
And then, 'twas otherwise!

As carbon in the coal
And carbon in the gem
Are one, and yet — the former
Were dull for diadem.

I rose, and all was plain, —
But when the day declined,
Myself and it in majesty
Were equally adorned.

The Grace that I was chose,
To me, surpassed the Crown
That was the Witness for the Grace, —
'Twas even that 'twas mine!

· LXXXIV ·

WITHOUT this there is nought;
All other riches be
As is the twitter of the bird
Heard opposite the sea.

I could not care to gain
A lesser than the whole;
For did not this include themselves,
As seams include the ball?

Or wished a way might be
My heart to subdivide,
'Twould magnify the gratitude
And not reduce the gold.

· LXXXV ·

IT would never be common more, I said,
Difference had begun;
Many a bitterness had been,
But that old sort was done.

Or if it sometimes showed, as 'twill
Upon the downiest morn,
Such bliss had I for all the years
'Twould give an easier pain.

I'd so much joy I told it red
Upon my simple cheek;
I felt it publish in my eye,
'Twas needless any speak.

I walked as wings of body bore,
The feet I former used
Unnecessary now to me
As boots would be to birds.

I put my pleasure all abroad,
I dealt a word of gold
For every creature that I met,
And dowered all the world.

When suddenly my riches shrank!
A goblin drank my dew —
My palaces dropped tenantless —
Myself was beggared too.

I clutched at sands — I groped at shapes —
I touched the tops of films,
I felt the wilderness roll back
Along my golden lines.

The sack cloth hangs upon the nail,
The frock I used to wear,
But where my moment of brocade —
My drop of India?

· LXXXVI ·

THEY put us far apart,
As separate as Sea
And her unsown peninsula, —
We signified "These see."

They took away our eyes,
They thwarted us with guns, —
"I see Thee" each responded straight,
Through telegraphic signs.

With dungeons they devised,
But through their thickest skill
And their opaquest adamant
Our Souls saw just as well.

They summoned us to die.
With sweet alacrity
We stood upon our stapled feet
Condemned, but first to see!

Permission to recant,
Permission to forget, —
We turned our backs upon the Sun
For perjury of that!

Not either noticed Death,
Of Paradise aware, —
Each Other's face was all the Disc
Each Other's setting saw.

·LXXXVII·

TO make one's toilette, after Death
Has made the toilette cool
To only taste we care to please,
Is difficult; and still —

That's easier than braid the hair
And make the bodice gay,
When eyes that fondled it are wrenched
By Decalogues away.

·LXXXVIII·

IT might have been lonelier
Without the loneliness;
I'm so accustomed to my fate
Perhaps the other — peace —

Would interrupt the dark,
And crowd the little room —
Too scant, by cubits, to contain
The Sacrament of Him.

I am not used to hope:
It might intrude upon —
Its sweet parade blaspheme the place
Ordained to suffering.

It might be easier
To fail with land in sight
Than gain my blue peninsula —
To perish — of delight.

·LXXXIX·

FORGET? The lady with the amulet
Forget she wore it at her heart
Because she breathed against?
Was treason 'twixt?

Deny? Did rose her bee
For privilege of play
Or will of butterfly
Or opportunity, her Lord away?

The lady with the amulet will fade;
The bee in mausoleum laid
Discard his bride;
But longer than the little rill

That cooled the forehead of the hill
While other went the sea to fill,
And other went to turn the mill,
I'll do thy will.

· XC ·

I WOULD die to know — 'tis a trifling knowledge —
News-boys salute the door, carts joggle by,
Morning's bold face stares in the window, —
Were but mine the charter of the least fly!

Houses hunch the house with their brick shoulders,
Coals from a rolling load rattle — how near
To the very square his foot is passing —
Possibly this moment! — while I dream here.

· XCI ·

LET us play yesterday —
I the girl at school,
You and Eternity
The untold tale.

Easing my famine
At my lexicon,
Logarithm had I for drink —
'Twas a dry wine.

Somewhat different must be
Dreams tint the sleep,
Cunning reds of morning
Make the blind leap.

Still at the egg-life,
Chafing the shell,
When you troubled the ellipse —
And the bird fell.

Manacles be dim, they say,
To the new free, —
Liberty commoner
Never could to me.

'Twas my last gratitude
When I slept at night,
'Twas the first miracle
Let in with the light.

Can the lark resume the shell
Easier for the sky?
Wouldn't bonds hurt more
Than yesterday?

Wouldn't dungeons sorer grate
On the man — free —
Just long enough to taste —
Then doomed new?

God of the manacle
As of the free,
Take not my liberty
Away from me!

· XCII ·

A SINGLE screw of flesh
Is all that pins the soul
That stands for Deity to mine,
Upon my side the vale.

Once witnessed of the gauze,
Its name is put away
As far from mine as if no plight
Had printed yesterday

In tender, solemn alphabet.
My eyes just turned to see —
When it was smuggled by my sight
Into Eternity.

More hands to hold! — these are but two —
One more new mailéd nerve
Just granted for the peril's sake —
Some striding giant love

So greater than the gods can show
They shrink before the clay,
That not for all their heaven can boast
Will let its keepsake go.

· XCIII ·

IF he dissolve — then there is nothing more,
Eclipse at midnight — it was dark before!

Sunset at Easter — blindness on the dawn,
Faint Star of Bethlehem gone down!

· XCIV ·

I CROSS till I am weary
A mountain in my mind,
More mountains, then a sea, more seas,
And then a desert find.

And my horizons blocks
With steady drifting grains,
Of unconjectured quantity —
As Asiatic rains.

Nor this defeat my pace —
It hinder from the West
But as an enemy's salute
One hurrying to rest.

What merit had the goal
Except there intervene
Faint doubt, and far competitor
To jeopardize the gain?

At last the grace in sight,
I shout unto my feet —
Offer them the half of Heaven
The instant that We meet.

They strive — and yet delay;
They perish. Do we die —
Or is this Death's experiment
Reversed in Victory?

·XCV·

WE prove it now, whoever doubt,
We stop to prove it, now.
Make haste the scruple! Death be scant
For opportunity!

The River reaches to my feet,
And yet my heart be dry!
Oh Lover, Life could not convince,
Might Death enable Thee!

The River reaches to my breast, —
Still, still my hands above
Proclaim with their remaining might —
Dost recognize the Love?

The River reaches to my mouth, —
Remember, when the Sea
Swept by my searching eyes the last —
Themselves were quick with Thee!

PART SEVEN

ADDITIONAL POEMS

(Published under the Title, "Unpublished Poems")

FOUR

· XCVI ·

SEXTON! my Master's sleeping here,
Pray lead me to his bed!
I came to build the Bird's nest
And sow the early seed,

That when the snow creeps slowly
From off his Chamber door,
Daisies point the way there,
And the Troubadour.

· XCVII ·

IF I could bribe them by a Rose
I'd bring them every flower that grows
From Amherst to Cashmere!
I would not stop for night or storm,
Or frost or death or Anyone,
My business were so dear!

If they would linger for a Bird,
My tambourine were soonest heard
Among the April woods!
Unwearied all the summer long
Only to break in wilder song
When winter shook the boughs!

What if they hear me! Who shall say
That such an importunity
May not at last avail?
That weary of this Beggar's face
They may not finally say Yes,
To drive me from the Hall?

· XCVIII ·

TOO little way the house must lie
From every human heart
That holds in undisputed lease
A white inhabitant.

Too narrow is the right between,
Too imminent the chance;
Each consciousness must emigrate
And lose its neighbor once.

· XCIX ·

'TIS well, the looking back on grief,
To re-endure a day
We thought the mighty funeral
Of all conceived by joy;

To recollect how busy grass
Did meddle, one by one,
Till all the grief with Summer waved --
And none could see the stone.

And though the woe you have today
Be larger, as the sea
Exceeds its unremembered drop —
They prove one chemistry.

· C ·

THE months have end, the years a knot
No power can untie,
To stretch a little further
A skein of misery.

The Earth lays back these tired lives
In her mysterious drawers
Too tenderly that any doubt
An ultimate repose;

The manner of the children
Who weary of the day,
Themselves the noisy plaything
They cannot put away.

· CI ·

BEREAVEMENT in their death to feel
Whom we have never seen,
A vital kinsmanship impart
Our souls and theirs, between.

For strangers — strangers do not mourn —
There be Immortal friends
Whom Death see first. 'Tis news of this
That paralyze ourselves.

Who, vital only to our thought,
Such presence bear away
In dying, 'tis as if our souls
Absconded suddenly.

· CII ·

'TWAS awkward, but it fitted me,
An ancient-fashioned heart;
Its only love its steadfastness,
In change unerudite.

It only swerved as do the suns
For merit of return,
Or birds confirmed perpetual
By alternating zone.

I only have it not tonight
In its established place
For technicality of Death —
Omitted in the lease.

·CIII·

BECAUSE 'twas riches I could own,
Myself had earned it me,
I knew the dollars by their names,
It feels like poverty

An earldom out of sight to hold,
An income in the air.
Possession has a sweeter chink
Unto a miser's ear.

·CIV·

TAKE your Heaven further on —
This to Heaven divine has gone.
Had you earlier blundered in
Possibly e'en you had seen
An Eternity put on.
Now to ring a door beyond
Is the utmost of your hand.
To the Skies apologize —
Nearer to your courtesies
Than this sufferer polite
Dressed to meet you, see — in white!

· CV ·

IT knew no medicine —
It was not sickness, then,
Nor any need of surgery —
And therefore, 'twas not pain.

It moved away the cheeks
A dimple at a time,
And left the profile plainer;
And in the stead of bloom

It left the little tint
That never had a name —
You've seen it on a cast's face;
Was Paradise to blame

If, her sweet door ajar,
Temerity drew near
And sickened ever afterward
For whatsoe'er it saw?

· CVI ·

HER smile was shaped like other smiles:
The dimples ran along —
And still it hurt you, as some bird
Did hoist herself to sing —

Then recollect a ball she got,
And hold upon the twig,
Convulsive, while the music cracked —
Like beads among the bog.

But this one wears a merriment
So patient, like a pain
Fresh gilded to elude the eyes
Unqualified to scan.

·CVII·

No notice gave she but a change, —
No message but a sigh —
For whom — the time did not suffice
That she should specify.

She was not warm, though Summer shone,
Nor scrupulous of cold,
Though rime by rime the steady Frost
Upon her bosom piled.

Of shrinking ways, forebore her fright
Though all the village looked,
But held her gravity aloft
And met the gaze direct.

Then when adjusted like a seed
In careful fitted ground
Unto the Everlasting Spring,
And hindered but a mound

Her warm return, if so she chose,
And we, imploring, drew, —
Removed our invitation by
As some she never knew.

·CVIII·

These saw vision, latch them softly;
These held dimples, smooth them slow;
This addressed departing accents —
Quick, sweet mouth, to miss them so.

This we stroked, unnumbered satin;
Those we held among our own —
Fingers of the slim Aurora
Not so arrogant this noon.

These adjust that ran to meet us,
Pearl for stocking — pearl for shoe;
Paradise the only palace
Fit for her reception — now.

·CIX·

TO die takes just a little while —
They say it doesn't hurt;
It's only fainter by degrees,
And then — it's out of sight.

A darker ribbon for a day,
A crape upon the hat;
And then the pretty sunshine comes
And helps us to forget

The absent, mystic Creature,
That but for love of us,
Had gone to sleep that soundest time
Without the weariness.

·CX·

HER sweet turn to leave the homestead
Came the darker way;
Carriages, be sure, and guests too, —
But for holiday

'Twas more pitiful endeavour
Than did swelling sea
O'er the curls attempt to caper
It had cast away.

Never bride had such assembling;
Never kinsman kneeled
To salute so fair a forehead,
Garlanded indeed.

Fitter feet of Her before us,
Than whatever brow
Art of snow or trick of lily
Ever could endow.

Of her father whoso claim Her,
He shall seek as high
As the palm that serve the desert
To obtain the sky.

He must pass the crystal angle
That obscure Her face;
He must have achieved in person
Equal Paradise.

Distance be Her only motion;
If 'tis Nay — or Yes —
Acquiescence or demurrer —
Whosoever guess.

· CXI ·

SHE lay as if at play
Her life had leaped away
Intending to return —
But not so soon.

Her merry arms half dropt
As if for lull of sport
An instant had forgot
The trick to start.

Her dancing eyes ajar
As if their owner were
Still sparkling through
For fun at you.

Her morning at the door,
Devising, I am sure,
To force her sleep —
So light, so deep.

·CXII·

SHE bore it till the simple veins
Traced azure on her hand,
Till pleading, round her quiet eye,
The purple crayons stand;

Till daffodils had come and gone,
I cannot tell the sum,
And then she ceased to bear it —
And with the Saints sat down.

No more her patient figure
At twilight soft to meet,
No more the timid bonnet
Upon the village street,

But crowns instead and courtiers, —
And in the midst so fair
Whose but her shy immortal face
Of whom we're whispering here!

·CXIII·

THIS heart that broke so long —
These feet that never flagged —
This faith that watched for Star in vain
Give gently to the Dead.

Hound cannot overtake the hare
That fluttered panting here —
Nor any school-boy rob the nest
Tenderness builded there.

·CXIV·

SHE'S happy, with a new content
That feels to her like Sacrament.
She's busy, with an altered care,
As just apprenticed to the Air.

She's tearful, if she weep at all,
For blissful causes, — most of all
That Heaven permit so meek as she
To such a Fate to minister.

·CXV·

SHE staked her feathers, gained an arc,
Debated, rose again, —
This time beyond the inference
Of Envy — or of Men.

And now among circumference
Her steady boat be seen —
At ease among the billows
As the bough where she was born.

·CXVI·

THE morning after woe,
'Tis frequently the way,
Surpasses all that rose before
For utter jubilee;

As Nature did not care
And piled her blossoms on,
The further to parade a joy
Her victim stared upon.

The birds declaim their tunes,
Pronouncing every word
Like hammers. Did they know they fell
Like Litanies of lead

On here and there a creature,
They'd modify the glee
To fit some Crucificial clef,
Some key of Calvary!

·CXVII·

UNIT, like Death, for whom?
True — like the Tomb
Who tells no secret
Told to him.

The Grave is strict —
Tickets admit
Just two — the Bearer
And the Borne —

And seat just One.
The Living tell
The Dying but a syllable;
The coy Dead — none.

·CXVIII·

IT was a grave, yet bore no stone,
Enclosed 'twas not by rail;
A consciousness its acre,
It held a human soul.

Entombed by whom, for what offense,
If home — or foreign born,
Had I the curiosity
'Twere not appeased of Man.

Till Resurrection I must guess,
Denied the small desire
A rose upon its ridge to sow,
Or palliate a briar.

· CXIX ·

BETWEEN my Country
And the Others
There is a Sea —
But flowers
Negotiate between us
As ministry.

(*In the old grave-yard*)

· CXX ·

THE color of the grave is green, —
The outer grave, I mean, —
You would not know it from the field
Except it own a stone.

It helps the Fond to find it,
Too infinite asleep
To stop and tell them where it is,
But just a daisy deep.

The color of the grave is white,—
The Winter grave, I mean, —
You would not know it from the drifts
In Winter, till the Sun

Has furrowed out the aisles, —
Then higher than the land
The little dwelling houses rise
Where each has left a Friend.

The color of the grave within, —
The duplicate, I mean, —
Not all the snows could make it white —
Not all the Summers, green.

You've seen the color, maybe,
Upon a bonnet bound,
When that you met it with before,
The ferret cannot find.

·CXXI·

A FIRST mute coming
In the stranger's house —
A first fair going
When the bells rejoice —

A first exchange
Of what hath mingled firm
For lot — exhibited
To Faith alone.

·CXXII·

PUT up my lute — what of my music!
Since the sole ear I cared to charm
Passive as granite laps my music,
Sobbing will suit as well as psalm!

Would but the Memnon of the desert
Teach me the strain that vanquished him
When he surrendered to the Sunrise —
Maybe that would awaken them!

·CXXIII·

NO man can compass a despair.
As round a goalless road
No faster than a mile at once
The traveller proceed —
Unconscious that the sun
Be setting on his progress —
So accurate the one
At estimating pain
Whose own has just begun.
His ignorance the Angel
That pilot him along.

·CXXIV·

GOOD to have had them lost
For news that they are saved!
The nearer they departed us
The nearer they — restored —

Shall stand to our right hand.
Most precious are the Dead, —
Most precious those that turned to go,
Then thought of us — and stayed!

·CXXV·

THE province of the Saved
Should be the art to save
Through skill obtained within themselves.
The science of the grave

No man can understand
But he that hath endured
The dissolution in himself;
That man be qualified

To certify Despair
To those who, failing new,
Mistake Defeat for Death each time —
Till acclimated to.

·CXXVI·

DESPAIR'S advantage is achieved
By suffering, — despair
To be assisted of reverse
One must have previous borne.

The worthiness of suffering,
Like the excellence of Death,
Is ascertained by tasting —
As can no other mouth

Of savours make us conscious,
As did ourselves partake.
Affliction feels impalpable
Until ourselves are struck!

·CXXVII·

THAT after horror that was Us —
That passed the mouldering pier
Just as the granite crumb let go,
Our savior by a hair —

A second more had dropped too deep
For fisherman to plumb —
The very profile of the thought
Puts recollection numb!

The possibility to pass,
Without a moment's bell,
Into Conjecture's presence —
Is like a face of steel

That suddenly looks into ours
With a metallic grin, —
The cordiality of Death
Who drills his welcome in.

· CXXVIII ·

'TIS so appalling it exhilarates!
So over-horror it half captivates!
The Soul stares after it — secure,
To know the worst leaves no dread more.
To scan a ghost is faint,
But grappling conquers it.
How easy torment now —
Suspense kept sawing so!
The truth is bald and cold,
But that will hold.
If any are not sure,
We show them prayer —
But we who know
Stop hoping now.
Looking at Death is Dying —
Just let go the breath,
And not the pillow at your cheek
So slumbereth.
Others can wrestle, yours is done,
And so of woe bleak dreaded, come —
It sets the fright at liberty,
And terror's free —
Gay, ghastly holiday!

·CXXIX·

THE test of Love is Death,
Our Lord "so loved", it saith;
What Largest Lover hath —
Another doth!

If smaller patience be
Through less infinity,
If bravo sometimes swerve
Through fainter nerve,

Accept its most —
And overlook the dust.
Last, least,
The Cross' request!

·CXXX·

A NEARNESS to Tremendousness
An Agony procures,
Affliction ranges Boundlessness.
Vicinity to laws
Contentment's quiet suburb, —
Affliction cannot stay
In acre or location —
It rents Immensity.

·CXXXI·

ONLY God possess the secret,
Only God!
The Jehovahs are no babblers.
Unto God
God the Son disclose it,
Still secure.
God the Spirit's honor
Equal sure.

APPENDIX

·I·

(*Sent at Christmas with an iced cake*)

THE Savior must have been a docile Gentleman
To come so far, so cold a night
For little fellow men.
The road to Bethlehem —
Since He and I were boys —
Has levelled — but for that 'twould be
A rugged billion miles.[1]

·II·

(*With a bit of Pine*)

A FEATHER from the whippoorwill
That everlasting sings,
Whose galleries are sunrise,
Whose stanzas are the spring,
Whose emerald nest the ages spin
With mellow murmuring thread,
Whose beryl egg what schoolboys hunt
In "recess" overhead![2]

·III·

THERE are two ripenings —
One of sight, whose forces
Spheric wind,
Until the velvet product
Drops, spicy, to the ground.

[1] Published on page 60 of the "Life and Letters."
[2] Published on page 266 of the "Life and Letters."

A homelier maturing,
The process in the burr —
That teeth of frosts
Alone disclose
On far October air.[1]

·IV·

THE zeros taught us phosphorus,
We learned to like the fire
By handling glaciers when a boy,
And tinder guessed by power
Of opposite to equal ought,
Eclipses suns imply,
Paralysis our primer numb
Unto vitality.[2]

·V·

JUST once! Oh, least request!
Could Adamant refuse
So small a grace
So scanty put —
Such agonizing terms?
Would not a God of Flint
Be conscious of a sigh
As down His Heaven
Dropt, remote,
"Just once! Sweet Deity?"[3]

[1] Published on page 207 of the "Life and Letters."
[2] Published on page 227 of the "Life and Letters."
[3] Published on page 256 of the "Life and Letters."

NOTE

All poems in the appendix are reproduced from the original manuscripts of Emily Dickinson's poems, not as quoted by her in her letters.

INDEX OF FIRST LINES